Lust

WESLEYAN BOOKS BY MICHAEL EIGEN

Ecstasy (2001)

Rage (2002)

The Sensitive Self (2004)

Emotional Storm (2005)

OTHER BOOKS BY MICHAEL EIGEN

The Psychotic Core (1986)

Coming Through the Whirlwind (1992)

The Electrified Tightrope (ed. Adam Phillips, 1993)

Reshaping the Self (1995)

Psychic Deadness (1996)

The Psychoanalytic Mystic (1998)

Toxic Nourishment (1999)

Damaged Bonds (2001)

Lust

MICHAEL EIGEN

Wesleyan University Press MIDDLETOWN, CONNECTICUT

Published by Wesleyan University Press,
Middletown, CT 06459
www.wesleyan.edu/wespress
© 2006 by Michael Eigen
All rights reserved
Designed by Richard Hendel
Set in Monotype Centaur and Minion
by BW&A Books, Inc.
Printed in the United States of America

Cataloging-in-Publication Data appear on
the last printed page of this book.
ISBN 0-8195-6808-2 (cloth)
ISBN 0-8195-6809-0 (pbk.)

5 4 3 2 1

Desires are nourishing, like ocean waves. They can kill you, thrill you, fill your heart with beauty, feel good all over. And most of our desires have laws that go with them.

Pleasure almost always tends to be more than itself. It spreads through body and self, so that a good experience confirms one's sense of self, makes one feel better as a person. Pleasure is associated with the goodness of life. It is a signifier of the bounty of life and is associated with an array of states leading to the ecstatic. In lust one is not merely after pleasure but after what pleasure gives one or where pleasure leads.

—Adapted from Toxic Nourishment

You open your hand and satisfy the desire of every living being.
—Psalm 145:16

CONTENTS

Introduction

Lust, one of the seven deadly sins, is part of what gives life luster, heightening existence. It can be degrading and part of a will to power, an assertion of dominance. As an act of self-affirmation, it can take many forms. It can foster links between people or destroy links. It melds generative and destructive modes of linking into kaleidoscopic amalgams, some finer, some grosser.

Traditionally, its link to sin involves the problem of control. Lust, as something out of control, disregards the rights of others. It is sin as trespass, as violation. The fact that we violate each other in many ways, and violation begins in infancy, gives lust as trespass special meaning. It carries an affective loading that compresses many kinds of violation into vivid sexual images. In a way, lust works overtime for personality, attempting to soothe, bypass, triumph over trauma, while causing further trauma of its own.

Lust has been associated with acts that keep the species going, disregarding the lives of individuals. At the same time, it has also been associated with individuality, ranging from the intimate experience of pleasure to capriciously or willfully breaking rules in the service of desire. Desire is species generic, carrying individuals in its wake, while also defining the taste, thrust, and direction of personal choice and style. Lust sticks its tongue out at social rules that limit it. One rides lust to freedom, often discovering that forces one fails to grasp rule one's bid for autonomy. The devil has sometimes been an image for this ambivalence, a symbol of evil disregard of others and a rebellious refusal to be shackled by deadening standards. Since childhood I've wondered why "evil" is "live" backward. Why is it that people are so afraid of living, so much so that the devil comes to be a symbol of aliveness? Lust plays no small role in this fear.

Mutual lust sometimes brings life to new places, opens heavens as well as hells. There is the possibility that pleasure, bliss, joy raise existence, take one out of oneself, give one more to oneself, affirm life's thrill. There is, after all, the thrill of being alive, of consciousness, of sensing, and lust stokes, revs up, gives impetus to this secret we all share. Life gets our attention in a special way through lust, makes us aware of itself, shakes us, arouses us to extra appreciation of the fact that we are here. Through the discovery that pleasure and its pursuit cause problems as well as satisfactions, lust becomes a challenge, a spur to address and learn something about our problematic nature. Its peaks and fusions of sensation, emotion, and will spill over into appreciative awe and mystery, adding to the taste and feel of life.

The method of this book is similar to that of my earlier books *Rage* and *Ecstasy*. My approach is to vary aspects of lust, moments of lust in different contexts, and dialogue with different approaches to lust. A good way to read this book is to find fragments that do something for you and stick with them. I mean this book to speak from self to self, make direct emotional transmissions, open possibilities of experience. My intent is not to control or dissolve lust but to vary it in reflective imagination and see what happens when it enters larger associative tapestries. These tapestries are necessarily selective, as I draw from personal experience, art, cinema, literature, psychoanalysis, religion, biology, and history.

Psychoanalysis teaches that lust is not unitary but made up of many impulses, sensations, feelings. Desire is made of many desires. Everything is partial, awash in subcomponents, subprocesses. Touch any desire, any component of lust, and a sea of experience opens. What seems unified for the moment, from the inside or outside, is filled with threads to pull, some more familiar, some as yet untouched. To get close to, feel out, work with different areas of experience commingles what is known with the uncreated. Freud calls consciousness a kind of psychic sense organ. For me, there is something I like to call "psychic taste buds." Our taste of the psyche, the taste of experience, is capable of growth. In important ways, how we taste to ourselves and each other has a lot to do not only with sensation, but also with how we live together, the quality of being.

Lust

Lust—overwhelming desire. To have, to possess, to enjoy. Dictionaries also say "excessive," as in excessive bodily appetite. Associated with vigor, life drive. Linked to the pleasure of the senses but also the will: lust for power.

A luster is one who lusts. No accident that it is linked with light, shining, radiance. Brilliance—associated with sex, power, fame. Intense longing, hunger—base, divine, devouring. *Zohar*, an important Kaballistic text means shining, splendor, brilliance, radiance. Fire below, fire above.

Many, many times in the midst of orgasm I see Light. Light everywhere. Light flowering out of sensation peaks, dancing with glee through many tufts of body. Body lights. Artists delineate glows, corporeal and spiritual. Keith Herring paints penises shining like light bulbs. Physical sensation lighting up, spreading light, radiant pulsations.

Lust enlarges, enriches, makes life taste good. Lust damages and grows from damage. Grows from power. Grows from fame. Grows from muddy festering in hidden swamps.

Everything is composite, made up of this and that. Lust is no exception. It may feel unitary for moments but on inspection yields many strings to pull. Lacan tells us learning plays an important role, that we would not know what to do if not for instruction: "The human being has always to learn from scratch from the Other what one must do as man or as woman." There is more to lust than a running off of mute instinct. For psychoanalysts, lust and desire are complicated.

In school I studied experiments in which chimpanzees with bad mothers or no mothers grew up to have bad sex or no sex. These chimps grew up to be less social, more withdrawn, more angry. Is sex, then, partly related to parenting, part of social being: the kind of sex you have reflects the kind of chimp you are? But isn't there something about sex itself that is disruptive? Doesn't it cause fights between partners, between competitors?

It can't be simple for people. Lacan speaks of "human beings." Beings for whom sex is mediated by symbols, beings for whom sex has meaning, many meanings.

It is said that Descartes was turned on by cockeyed women because he had a cockeyed nurse when he was little. Quite a literal, reductive instance of Freud's belief in a link between our parents and what our sex life is like.

But we are putting the cart before the horse, jumping where there is no place to land. It is time to turn a kaleidoscope, our lustoscope, and see some of the designs it forms from turn to turn.

When is lust lust? When is lust something else? When is lust lust *and* something else? A woman patient decides that her therapist is the man for her. She opens herself. He is the only man with whom she feels so open. At last, a man she can be with.

To him she looks beautiful, ever more beautiful. She is promise, she is heart. She is the Real.

Home is horror. Screaming, fighting, a rats' nest. His wife's face pinches him with its thin, tight lips. Like above, below; like below, above: thin, tight, cunt. She is oriented toward getting through the day. Taking care of chores. Business: the business of living. Nothing juicy. I've heard people say that marriage is a sexy business, but not for them.

He uses the word "business" a lot: "My marriage is a business deal." He cares for his wife as a person, so he says. He's crazy about his kids. But it is hell, and his patient is the Garden of Eden, serpent and Eve and apple rolled into one. Can he be Adam? Dare he?

They feel an ineluctable draw to each other. He thinks of her throughout the day, masturbates with her image in mind in the night. He feels her in his belly, in his heart. He chews on her. Succulence. Everything his marriage isn't. Everything he hoped it would be.

He speaks of intense conflict between marriage and lover. He is in pain. He fears hurting his wife and children. He does not want to be without his children.

His patient stops therapy, calls him, invites him to her place. He does not go. She stops calling and waits. Six months later she calls for an appointment. She is doing well but misses him. She invites him to stay with her. They touch. Feeling grows stronger. He feels alive for the first time in years.

Will he be brave enough? He sits with his patients and feelings stream through him. Life is happening. He thought it was closed to him, something to get through, a dead sea of chores.

He is lighter, even with heavy pain. Magnetic pull of something sweet and full moving toward climax. He tells me it is almost time.

A year later I get a note. He has never been happier. This *is* what he imagined life *could* be but feared it would not be for him.

You could say he escaped reality. You could say he found it. Reality is more than the sum of thoughts and words. Yet didn't image, thought, words play a role in leading him to the Real? The Real of love. One who wanted him, who opened. One who opened him, at last.

His wife accused him of breaking the only real thing she had, their family, their real family. She lectured, accused, bossed: can't he see that this is what *real* life is like? Work, taking care of things! Responsibility! Can't he see they had something special?

In his girlfriend's apartment, his former patient's, his lover's —his sweetheart's place. So this is what the valentines of popular culture are about! My God, these things people joke and sing about, write poems and make movies about—they exist. All the references and pictures of hearts, the heart of life. Hearts swimming. Cupid. Amor. My God, they're real!

~~~ Such feeling blunts the pain of feeling. There were moments when the agony of the injury he inflicted came home. He could bear only so much before rationalizing his children's wounds: is living in a dead and bitter environment good for kids? Having two corpses for parents, two antagonists? What kind of flowers grow with such ghastly nourishment?

At least the time he spends with them now is better than time spent with the sickly desert he was before. At least now they have moments glimpsing sunlight, moments of being with a father who is alive.

~~~ What did therapy do? He thanked me for giving him a place to come and deposit himself and talk himself out, hear himself, feel himself. I wondered, too, if he meant a place to deposit his pain, to hold his pain. Did talking about his pain relieve him of the necessity of feeling it? Did it allow him to make room for it in a larger vision? Talking about his desire did not take the wind out his sails. It distilled his desire, his longing, his pulse. Is it different for pain? Talking about it diminishes it?

I got the sense he knew what he wanted to do from the first moment he came in my door—he *knew* what he was going to do. It was only a matter of time. Therapy as catapult, a place to build momentum.

Can a therapist be neutral? Would I do what he did? I have stayed with my family through thick and thin. But then, my wife isn't like his, not the way he makes her sound. The polarity between dryness and succulence was not as pronounced in my life as in his.

Is there an ethical position I'm supposed to take? What am I supposed to be doing? With all my might I try to keep things open, as he vacillates, veering back and forth, making himself feel better about what he is preparing to do.

He breaks appointments, stretches out meetings intermittently over months. Maybe he fears that if we go too deep, he will not go through with his plan. He will not like what he sees. He uses therapy as an alibi, an excuse for lust. A convoluted way of giving himself permission to do what he will do. Therapy as part of a foregone conclusion rather than an investigation. Sometimes there is not much more to do than wish the other well.

In a dream I hear a voice: "The pain he caused would always be with him. But the joy in living he felt was something no pain could take away."

My patient opted for beauty, for promise, experience in which lust, pleasure, joy, spirit commingle. Heart, face, genital connection, lust uniting with heaven, heavenly lust, perhaps a kind of love (Eros, that god!). The brutal was relegated to family, the place he was getting out of. You might guess there was repetition, that his father left him when he was a child. Pain passes through generations. He imagines this pain will be left behind by his leaving, starting anew. The pain will be passed to his children: let them deal with it. A growing debt future generations cannot catch up with.

There are other scenarios—for example, one of opposition: a refusal to subjugate himself to the living death his parents endured. He can be part of a new generation with more emphasis on self, the right to be. It is immoral to suppress one's best possibilities. To stagnate and decay in oppressive conditions is a sin against life. An "ethics" of renewal demands making the most of what life offers. In my patient's case, life is offering a chance at greater happiness. A brutal shadow attaches to lustful sensitivity, even when the latter is redemptive.

Of the various forms of lust, you'd think the least ambiguous would be rape. One person's lust satisfying itself without regard for the feelings of the other. What could be clearer? Yet the slightest meditation on literature, art, or history opens snake pits.

The rape of the Sabine women, depicted by Bologna, Rubens, Poussin, Picasso, mentioned by Plutarch. Rape linked to political calculation. Rome needs sons to build power. The Sabines are invited to a feast in honor of Neptune, making it easier for Roman men to take Sabine women. Women's pained faces and struggling bodies, men grabbing them, fights breaking out between warriors. Such an ancient theme. Rubens depicts the Romans defeating the Sabines when the latter try to avenge this breach of hospitality. It is also said that war was averted by the Sabine women reconciling with their captors. Force wins not only compliance but assent. To reconcile with one's rapist, fantasy and social reality.

I have seen paintings of this rape since my childhood. Is it wrong to call it rape? Wrong to call it lust? Lust for power, sex in service of empire, sexual politics, a matter of having women bear babies to fatten armies? Lusts blur. Sex and power fuse and feed each other. My young mind stamped with images of military might melded with women's bodies, thrills of triumph and agony, abduction as elemental, normative, compliance a mode of survival. Horrible play on words: surrender as brutal defeat, surrender as ecstatic opening. Primal words and images often fuse opposite meanings. Bologna's sculpture mixes armor and nakedness, intimacy and metal on flesh. Metal cutting into, subjugating flesh, flesh melting metal.

The Roman Neptune is a watered down version of the great Greek Poseidon. The former is a god of horses and games, images suitable for the pretext used to lure the Sabines. But underneath, at deeper levels, primordial rumblings of Poseidon continue, a god earlier than Zeus, stirring waters to calm or storm, lusting after women and goddesses, begetting monsters and springs, a god of oracles before Apollo, keeping Odysseus on the edge of disaster, a god of earthquakes as well as drowning. Horses pulled Poseidon's chariot and perhaps here, through horses, Romans sought to tame this vehicle of primordial forces, make him into a more political figure, something to control. Control: a great Roman theme amid the tumult. Chaos, chance, impulse vs. will and struggle, as if expanding empire will subjugate life.

In parlor astrology Neptune is a sign of dream, intuition, poetry, spirit. As if spiritual is something other than fierce fighting. A wish for peaceful growth rather than growth that rips. But if one seeks to channel Poseidon, one tries to channel something brutal, able to flare up any time, ready to go the wrong way, always dangerous. Poseidon represents force and will that will not be controlled, not in any final way, not for long.

Freud uses liquid and electrical images for libido as it changes form like the gods, mixing Poseidon, Zeus, and streaming hosts of characters. With "ego" comes military images, energy shaped into strategic battalions, force and intimacy between Eros and Mars.

It does not take much close observation to note that ego is a part of impulses the gods represent. There is little separation between ego and impulse in the behavior of gods. Impulse is filled with ego, ego with impulse. Calculation and drive go together in the quest for pleasure, power, and honor.

The *Iliad* begins nine years into a war occasioned by erotic theft, Paris's abduction of Helen, Menelaus's wife. Armies fighting over a woman? To right a wrong? An erotic pretext for political-military mania, vanity, honor? Gods, with their own wounded desires and grievances, are very much in the mix. Layers of motives around erotic nuclei, the latter seized by group and individual pride. Violation triggers violation, force meets force, momentum of sins of trespass.

Is lust always so triangular, so Oedipal—the other man, the other woman part of the structure of sexual appetite, nested in a primal triad, mother-father-child? A patient, after his wife died, spoke of dreams in which other men take her from him. The dream *is* anxiety substituted for grief: other men take his wife, he is losing her, she goes willingly, she is being violated. Force he fears he cannot control, the other's desire, the other's fate.

At the start of the *Iliad*, Achilles broods about the abduction of his favorite slave girl, Briseis, by Agamemnon, an ally. Ally and rival meld. Beset by one of the great funks of literature, Achilles refuses to fight, at great cost to his side. Briseis suffered greatly when taken by Achilles, who murdered her husband, friend, and brothers. But she did not find Achilles unpleasant, and the possibility of wedding a winner appealed to her.

Agamemnon loves his slave Amyntor more than his wife, something he will pay for when he returns home. His slave, at least in fantasy, gave him something his wife didn't. We will leave open what this mysterious X is.

Erotic theft within theft. Change within time. Helen becomes Helen of Troy, the wife of her Trojan man. In contrast, Odysseus remains faithful to his wife, Penelope, in his heart, and she to him, both dealing with other men or women in their own ways. At the end of the *Odyssey*, we are treated to a glimpse of their connection, as the couple feel their way back into each other, after Odysseus and his son kill Penelope's suitors, who had violated their home.

Literature warns that life is ever in danger of turning against itself, self against self, group against group. Much effort is required to avert disaster, although we are not sure what kind of effort this might be.

Homer tells us that life and growth are not possible without disaster, although we wish it otherwise. Is it jejune to think that, at least, we can try to make the most of what we can't avoid? The fact that lust goes with painful difficulties does not make it less attractive. The final picture of Odysseus with Penelope, after everything they have gone through, suggests a larger perspective.

The idea of making war because of violation attached to making love is ancient. Lust and purity, individual and group, heart, guts, genitals, politics, God—elements of the biblical mix. In one of the searing stories in Genesis that seem to be included almost in passing, Jacob buys land in Canaan from Hamor's sons and prepares to live in peace. Hamor is the Hiviite prince of the region, and the land that Jacob purchases is in an area presided over by one of Hamor's sons, Shechem. Jacob has just made peace with Esau and looks forward to a normal life tending flocks. Of course, normal life is not too normal in the Bible.

Peace has its moments but often is a buzzword. Like Laurel and Hardy saying, "What a beautiful day," the word "peace" almost signifies disaster. Biblical normality is strife torn, tends toward trouble, heartbreak. So much so that a special day, the Sabbath, was created in peace's honor, perhaps because it contrasts with much of life. It did not take long after Jacob settled in for peace to shatter.

As with so much biblical reality, it is difficult to pin down an exact cause, but lust plays a central role. Dinah, Leah and Jacob's daughter, went walking in the land to see the women. Shechem saw her and "took her and lay with her, forcing her. But his emotions clung to her—he loved her and spoke to her heart." A lot happens pretty quickly.

Commentators ask, why did Dinah go walking? A brash thing to do? A lure? Asking for trouble? Woman as active agent? Punished for boldness, inquisitiveness, for being alive? Venturing forth, like a man? She went to see the women of the land, check out the customs, get a feel for where she was, enlarge her sense of place, connection, orientation. Wasn't her little enclave enough?

It's not the first time curiosity met with punishment. Near the beginning of Genesis, God's voice goes out walking, sensing trouble.

Adam, Eve/Pandora, the serpent, the fruit, the bite, the taste. Sweet and bitter fruit, juicy, succulent. Lust for life and knowledge slide up and down sensory-feeling-mental scales. Past barriers and prohibitions, whirls of meaning, Faustian moments. The one thing you mustn't do, you do. Even God you don't listen to, especially God. A course of history is set: rulers want obedience: living breaks the seams. But who are rulers? The same who break the seams.

Command givers-obeyers-breakers. Clash of personality, clash within personality. Serpent mind: eat and be like gods, immortal, know what's good and bad. A promise that turns into its opposite: eat and know death, you are going to die. Eat and know. Eat and die. Lust and know. Lust and die. Eat life, eat death. Rise, fall. Fallible, gullible mortality, hungry for everything.

Everything!

Who is Dinah? What does she do? She is part of a play of forces that teases the edge of limits. Creative limits, creative edges, in myth and reality often somberly destructive. Death follows Orpheus and Eurydice, Tristan and Isolde, Romeo and Juliet, Othello and Desdemona, Lear, his kingdom, his daughters: dramas of body ego. Dramas of transcendental ego link serpent, Tiresias, Eve/Pandora, Shakespeare's fools, figures of mad wisdom, Kerouac's Dharma bums. Themes of recent French philosophy: transgression, excess.

Dinah goes out to the larger world and is raped. What gives Shechem the right, the authority? He is the boss of the town or sub-boss under his father. He can't and doesn't have to resist impulse, attraction, the pull, ardor. Lust often is portrayed as irresistible surge. Here the Bible suggests that privilege plays a role in irresistibility of impulse. The boss of the town does not have to do battle with himself. He can indulge himself. He has power. He can afford giving in to himself. He feels entitled.

A daughter of one of God's favorites meets a prince of privilege. Rape is not confined to privilege, of course. Poor people rape. Rape signifies power and powerlessness and slides across scales of might and deprivation. Power hierarchies exist for poor people and in the bedrooms of all people.

In the Shechem-Dinah scene, we have a sense of a man powerless against his urges who renders the woman powerless. Is it that man cannot bear woman's erotic power and by possessing her nullifies it: fulfillment as nullification? Is it that man cannot tolerate the buildup of erotic tension and seeks fast release? Perhaps, too, there is something deeper at stake: humanity's difficulty tolerating the buildup of experiential tension, the tendency to spill and get rid of rather than to process and digest.

Did Shechem follow his genitals, heart, eyes, arms, the need to have and possess? The phrasing of the Bible suggests that Shechem meant to satisfy his wish for Dinah and move on. He did not expect more to happen. "But his emotions clung to Dinah—he loved the girl." Surprised by affect, by love. One never knows in advance the outcome of an act. Often lust is satisfied and one moves on. But there are times lust opens worlds of feeling.

Shechem was in over his head. He thought he was pursuing a girl, a wife. He did not understand that he was also penetrating a group, a people, a nation. The sense of violation spreads and encompasses personal and communal dimensions. The meeting of Dinah and Shechem, whatever their individual predicament, also represents the interpenetration of groups.

An ominous tone is struck: Jacob heard that Shechem defiled his daughter but remained silent until his sons returned from the fields. The men agonize over a violation not only of Dinah but of Israel (34:5). Hamor, in apparent good faith, not only proposes marriage between Shechem and Dinah, but between his people and Jacob's: Settle here, intermarry, purchase land, raise families, do business, "give us your daughters and take our daughters for yourselves." Shechem, too, pleaded for Dinah as a wife, making a generous offering. Their requests seem eminently reasonable.

The Bible tells us that Jacob's sons—not Jacob—acted deceitfully.

They appeared to accept Hamor and Shechem's overtures, only on condition that Hiviite men get circumcised: "We can't give our sister to a man with foreskin!" Nor, by implication, any daughter of Israel. Hamor and Shechem accept, and while the Hiviite men recuperate, Shimon and Levi, Dinah's full brothers (sons of Leah), kill them all and take Dinah back. Jacob's other sons despoil the Hiviites' city "because they violated their sister."

Not a pleasant outcome for what seemed to Shechem a terrifically beautiful feeling.

It is a story in which no one is innocent, but it is not clear that the punishment fits the crime. Lest you think Hamor's offer merely generous, note that he tells his men, "All their animals and property—won't they become ours, part of our wealth, if they settle with us?" A certain self-interest, if not greed at the prospect of more wealth, graced the Hiviite appetite. We see, too, they kidnapped Dinah. The Bible does not tell us what Dinah felt. It only describes the men's intentions and reactions. Shechem spoke to Dinah's heart, but we do not hear how Dinah's heart responds.

Jacob rebuked Shimon and Levi for creating such trouble. He fears others will retaliate and destroy them, as they are a small group. But Shimon and Levi retort, "Should our sister be treated like a whore?" God tells Jacob to move on, and Jacob does, after acknowledging God and making sacrifices. Jacob and his family escape without trouble, as other groups steer clear of the crazy Hebrews for a time.

Far from this incident being a throw-away, it carries immense weight, with interpretative benefits still being reaped by us. The story is some kind of turning point (what Bible story isn't?). Soon afterward, Jacob's parents and his favorite wife, Rachel, die. Once more he receives God's blessing and a name change to Israel. His life is in God's hands more completely than ever, and the way is prepared for the story of Joseph in Egypt, the emergence of Moses, the giving of the Law. The story is shifting from Jacob to his sons, as it already shifted from Abraham and Isaac to Jacob. We know how important the slaughter of the Hiviites is, because Jacob cursed Shimon and Levi on his death bed: "Damned be their anger, their fury, their harshness." He condemns them for willful murders, yet he was silent when the scheme was hatched. In one man's act of lust and its consequences, everyone is implicated.

The story is packed with threads to tug on.

1. *Dinah's outgoing urge, élan, life-feeling.* Questions of innocence and guilt hover over biblical tales. Something bad is going to happen, and it's someone's fault. Often fault is distributed, impossible to disentangle. Many are implicated: Shechem, Hamor, Jacob, Shimon, Levi, Jacob's other sons. Guilt is individual *and* communal.

In addition to explicit characters in the story, there are implicit cast members: life and society being two of the most important. Each character mediates important life impulses, and each bears the weight of and mediates communal interests. The story relentlessly provokes meditation on human nature. Its extreme mixture of promise and violence gnaws at psychic bones and carries germs of a critique of life and society.

Our "innocent" élan, life drive, wish for more or other, curiosity, exploration, activity, play of sameness-difference—Dinah manifests it. She goes out from the same to the other. Not totally other: she wants to see the women of the land, the limit of what society permits.

There are perennial culture wars over human nature, its guilt and/or innocence. Nowadays diverse tendencies are seen as part of the plasticity that enables survival. Tension between self-interest and sacrifice, selfishness and benevolence, enriches textures of experience and behavior. A cultural thread with roots in antiquity tries to see beyond good and evil to how processes, forces, capacities stimulate and interpenetrate one another. Even so, there is disagreement over what constitutes these powers. For example, in early wars of depth psychology, Freud saw psychic energy as libidinal, whereas Jung believed it to be more general. Surely a woman can go out of her house without looking for sex. And if she does go out looking for sex, isn't that OK? It has taken a long time for the notion of female agency to have widespread political currency, but it has ancient tendrils, Dinah one of them in a circumscribed way. That she cannot walk safely in the land is a practical and ethical challenge to life and society.

The story reeks of the subjugation of women, limits on female rights and actions. Transgression and justice are in the hands of men, but women start the trouble. Dinah, Eve, Pandora, Helen. An object for men, doing double duty as object of desire and labor, a hard worker herself, yet blamed as an active agent, always at fault. In man's narrative, women can be counted on to cause trouble.

Dinah as carrier of life, life as fault, as trouble. You never know what will happen when you leave the house, although you may be more likely to be injured at home. Life subjects you to injury, but hiding doesn't help. In this regard, the story is about aliveness as trauma. Seeking life triggers injury.

The story offers no solution. Within the framework of the story, nothing works. Things go from bad to worse, subside, and the next story builds. Each story leaves residues, seeds, themes that are repeated and reworked. We see life working, life seeking life, causing or swerving from death, regrouping for another try.

There are many wonderful stories about going from smaller to bigger. Edwin A. Abbott's *Flatland*, for example, in which beings living in a two-dimensional plane can't imagine a three-dimensional world, nor those living in three dimensions imagine four. Intersection at boundaries is violent. In the Dinah story, life continues, goes to other places, moves from drama to drama. A tragic thread weaves its way through story after story, the élan Dinah embodies never free of consequences.

2. *Assimilation and purity: violence, violation, fertilization.* A problem highlighted in the Bible involves purity: ethical, tribal, and individual. The rape and courting of Dinah does not merely represent haphazard expression of one man's lust, but possible conjunction

of communities. Hamor intends (opportunistically) to absorb the Hebrews' riches, labor, and gene pool. The Hebrews express horror not only at the violation of a woman, but also at the potential violation of their tribe. Horror of assimilation, loss of identity, betrayal of ethnic and religious group calling.

With Moses, face-to-face vision melds with ethical and ritual commandments in mediating the holy bond that makes Israel a nation of priests. The godly bond mediated by earlier patriarchs becomes the site of new dramas of fidelity and betrayal, partly organized and mediated by formal laws. The purity of the godly bond includes maintenance via selective catastrophes, plagues, murder. Cut the sick branch off, preserve the holy core. Lust for purity.

Sons of Levi, for example, kill three thousand of their fellows, under Moses' directive, in response to the sin of the golden calf. Descendants of Levi, cursed by Jacob, are used by Moses in an act of purification, at once an atonement for sin and a consolidation of Mosaic power. Purification through earthquakes, flood, disease, conquerors, intragroup violence. Disaster as punishment, reminder, awakening.

There is a strong attempt in the Bible to make purification ritualistic and swerve from concrete horror—for example, substitute animal sacrifice and rules of purity for human injury. Unfortunately, such attempts tend to boomerang, since failures of observance may have destructive results. The urge to substitute psychospiritual drama for literal brutality perseveres to this day, but has not yet overcome a need for concrete violence. The biblical prophetic books diagnose the difficulty in terms of human intention and action: good vs. bad heart, mind, deed. Difficulty is located less in ritual obedience than in a more pervasive need to cultivate a caring and helping disposition, the challenge to be just to one another. To do justice to oneself, others, life. A challenge in the forefront of what exercises us today.

Today, discourse of purity-pollution remains virulent. Perhaps we will develop radar sensitivity to spot its work, whether subtle or gross. In my lifetime there was Hitler's Aryan purity, McCarthyism, and varieties of political, religious, ethnic, sexual fundamentalism with outbursts of destructive cleansing. At this moment, violent Islamic fundamentalists claim attention, frightening the world. Physical threats of Jewish fundamentalists are more local, confined to Israel/Palestine. The toll of Christian fundamentalism has yet to be reckoned, allied as it often is with bully politics and high-powered economic dominance.

Near the outset of the Holocaust there were religious Jews who thought they were being punished for sin. As the Holocaust went on, the enormity of horrors made it impossible to think that God could punish people this way. The ethical sense recoils at such a God. Yet God has a horrible history of destructive cleansing. A disappointed God nearly wiped out the entire human race in Noah's time. Difficulty compromising often signals destructive lust for purity. Association of purity with God has gotten us into endless trouble.

What is purity? Moses married a Midianite woman, whose father, Jethro, helped organize, if not create, Mosaic law. Freud was not the first to think that Moses might have been Egyptian. It is likely Hebrews adopted circumcision from others (also Egypt?) and skull caps from the Romans. Penetrate purity, you get hybrids. The Promised Land, the Holy Land is not the first tribal or national interest to be justified by appeal to God, nor will it be the last. The use of God to preserve a people, while people cross-fertilize. People kill to preserve purity. People kill for a fiction, but the bodies are real. Issues of power and purity mix. One of the great ironies or tricks of mind and body: fighting for purity often results in richer mixtures, as enemies or those behind enemy lines couple and cultures cross-pollinate.

But what if all human beings share in God's purity, purity of soul. Purity as universal spiritual vision, no one excluded. Can those who don't experience this purity exercise their right to be? A sense or attitude or principle of respect comes into play as a minimum practical or ethical grounding. Being who we are, we will fight over the nature of that respect, but perhaps agree to respect respect.

The Bible gains its power, partly, as a site of enormous tension. Often the idea of purity adds to the pool of meanness. Yet there is another thread, an appeal to something better. An appeal to care for others, to take care of others, to help. A tension between lust for violent cleansing and respect for life. More important than imaginary purity is the concrete reality of every human being. Is it merely an artifact of my profession to feel we all need each other's help—that, at any moment, any of us may be the one who gives?

To fight, to love, to lust, tension between strivings, to be holy, to sense the sacred everywhere, to degrade and be degraded, crawl in the dirt, to like being messy, down low.

Omnidirectional cravings—human beings.

What is the center of the Bible? Seeing God, seeing God. What does lust say to that?

"I see God, I see God."

To masturbate is to see God. All through childhood, I masturbated, day and night, many, many times a day, constantly.

This means I was a sick child. Only sick children masturbate all the time.

An attempt to soothe madness.

What age was I when I set fire to the woods in back of my house and the firemen came and I was questioned by them? I lived in fear they would give me to the police. I would be in jail at the age of seven because of displaced sick lust, frustrated love, a damaged soul. I was only beginning to realize that adults burnt forests, cities, bodies. You'd think sex was harmless, but there is not much evidence for that view.

When I grew up, I learned that I was not the only one who saw God when coming. Allen Ginsberg writes about a great revelation while reading William Blake and masturbating in his early twenties or late teens. I think he was a student at Columbia University. As I've gotten older, I've learned such experiences are not rare. Why does it still seem so secret, so taboo? What is so scary? That God is so near? That God is in the organs?

Sick kids don't have a latency period. Something I learned when I was studying psychoanalysis. Analysts claimed there is a period in childhood when kids aren't too interested in sex. They study numbers and other things in school.

Me? I was always getting crushes on girls I was afraid to have. Some I got to kiss. Some I kissed many times. That was what we did in those days, a lot of kissing.

When I was a teen in New Jersey, we'd drive on highway S-3 past Secaucus and smell the garbage dump while we kissed. The same place years later became Giants Stadium, where we were sure Jimmy Hoffa was buried, connected to the deaths of John and Bobby Kennedy.

My first vote: John Kennedy. I read he screwed lots of girls but got killed for other reasons. That's like thinking your hand or dick will fall off for touching yourself or your brain will get diseased (mad dick, mad cunt disease), but getting killed for fucking has got to be worse. You can get killed for fucking even if you're president. How dangerous can lust be? To have organs is already to risk murder.

It's tough when you're not a teen anymore, although as a teen I cried a lot. The pain was unbearable. Girls were fantasies, even when I touched them.

A blind kid who played piano insisted he could take bras off before girls knew it.

I counted on him to follow me when I jumped around on my sax, and he did. He never failed me. We got prizes for playing.

But I never believed him about girls. Not even a blind guy can get *that* good.

꙳ The one guy I almost believed took me to Philadelphia to meet girls. We were seniors in high school, and the next year I would go to the University of Pennsylvania and he to Temple University. I didn't quite get it. I didn't quite know what we were doing or supposed to do. I was used to not quite getting things. On the other hand, you never quite get used to not quite getting things even if befuddlement is something of a permanent state.

At supper all I could think of was whether to use a fork and knife or pick up the southern fried chicken (which I'd never seen or heard of before) with my fingers. My date and I were stiff together, and even though I used my fingers we were polite and said goodbye.

I waited for my friend while he did whatever he did in the bedroom with the supple girl who almost opened to him. Almost, almost, more than happened with me. Her parents weren't home. My hand chanced on a book by a lamp by e. e. cummings and I opened it and the flesh of language melted.

We went home to Passaic, where e. e. cummings did not exist, but a bleak, creepy, gritty magic hovers if you let it. My friend became a financial consultant, and I never stopped melting.

꙳ I'm thinking at a drive-in of a girl who everyone said did things. How did they do it? We did kissing but how much kissing can you do? An awful lot, I fear, too much, if there is a too much.

Years later I learn that she married my friend, who left her for his secretary. Left her with all their children. He looked happy when I met him, as if he had a secret habit of patting his own back. A grown-up. I was such a child.

In college a teacher told him not to be a writer, and he worked with money instead. I didn't know why he *should* or how he *could* listen to his teacher. If you have writing lust, you write. Did he sit on the hunger that writing is, give it up, lack it?

Years earlier we spit on the same stone and vowed to be buddies forever.

He did everything better than I. He was better at everything.

But the cruel fact was I could not be him.

When he was twelve, his maid jerked him off. We played monopoly and talked about it. Shame mixed with pride. Someday I'd get my chance too—but when?

All through high school I'd go late at night to the corner of Brook and Main Avenues, where I was sure I'd meet the girl who was waiting for me.

Sometimes I'd take a girl to the cemetery and stare at the moon, convinced it would come down and I would give it to her.

Sometimes I pretended to have a girlfriend named Betty, and I married a woman by that name thirty years later.

Lust and longing and loneliness went together a lot in my life.

At Penn a girl I struck out with introduced me to a friend of hers. "I think you might like each other," she said. How did she know! For a year we fucked and read Plato, saw Kandinsky and Klee, heard Ormandy conduct Bach, ate Chinese food, waffles and ice cream. Something finally happened!

One thing I learned about sex and love, besides the fact that I love sex: it can turn on a dime and be horrible. All kinds of pains and torments I never dreamt of made their appearance like weird plants in the cracks of my psyche. She changed schools, and I died and for the first time in my life got all A's.

~~~ God and lust have strong connections. Not just lust for bodies, or lust for souls. The fire of the personal is partly lust in the heart for something unfathomable, unquenchable, indecipherable, a thrilling, filling hunger that pierces bellies and genitals, leaves them wavering. The phrase "wavering in their wake" is acutely accurate because awakening is part of it.

~~~ I've heard many individuals link sex with disease. An eighty-year-old woman told me she remembers thinking sex made you sick. Not just venereal disease which was real enough (HIV entered our consciousness later). But sick to her stomach, sick in her head, sick in her chest. When she was a little girl, a teen, a young woman she associated sex with germs. Was it Milton Berle or some other comic who began his show, "Ladies and Germs!"? Sperm as germ but more. Somehow sex itself was viral. Dangerous. Placed you at risk.

Headaches, backaches, stomachaches, breathing difficulties—just thinking about sex did it. She never got married, never had children, but for many years had a very full social life.

She was not sexless. She had urges. High school and college fooling around, affairs as a young woman, living with a man for nearly two years. She actually liked sex once she got into it. But it was more a badge, a sign she was acceptable, doing what she should, what other young women did. A sign of prowess, ability, vitality, power. Still, she was frightened.

What scared her? Pleasure was part of it, pleasure that made her vulnerable, that would not stay localized and controlled. A man inside her spread pleasure through her, and she tightened. Fear of pleasure, yes, but also afraid of what a man would do to her life, to her personality. A man inside her life would make for unpredictable change. She feared sex would drive her crazy. Psychic germs, not just physical germs. A man stirring her up would bring her to places beyond what she dared to know, infect her with foreign feelings, with strange tumult. She became a prominent social figure but avoided life. Rather, she substituted one form of life for another—unfulfilled one way, fulfilled another. Who knows? Maybe she was better off than individuals I've seen who lived out passions but remained stunted as people.

She fought with the man she lived with for the two years they were together. "Being angry at this or that made it impossible to feel too much except the same narrow band. Neither of us were innocent. He used work as an escape and I'd find fault with him. Most of the time I hated myself and didn't know it. I was afraid of life and used anger to turn it on and off. Anger was my excuse.

"If I could do it over, I wouldn't do any better. I think I was determined to be by myself, to build a life around what I could take, to create the kind of contacts I could live with. Contacts at a friendly distance worked for me. I couldn't share my body, my insides. It has taken all these years to start touching places where no one gained admission."

She may have given up on sex, but sex did not give up on her. Sexual dreams came, sometimes strange sexual feelings. Several times she dreamt of little men, like dwarves. Walt Disney cartoons frightened her because of their body distortions. The seven dwarves, elfin creatures, Jiminy Cricket seemed to her something like rats to Freud's "rat man," afraid of penetration, disruption, madness. Getting stirred by something uncontrollable, scary diggers in filthy, collapsible mines. Suffocation with terror of permeability.

Now and then, sexual feelings came and she enjoyed them. Sometimes they were not too fraught with content, like a change of weather, a surprising breeze. A hint that sex is not always terrifying. At those moments, sex did not ask much of her, and she did not have to give too much.

In the past few years, an ominous symptom appeared. She began falling down, tripping, losing balance, knees buckling. Nothing showed up in exams except a weak knee, for which physical exercises were prescribed. "Old age," a doctor told her. "You're doing very well." But falling down to her meant she was losing orientation, vitality, whatever it took to carry one's own weight. In her life's observation, old people falling down meant deterioration, heading toward the end.

She dreamt of her parents in bed on a movie screen, as if she were in the audience. She was embarrassed. Her parents argued a lot when she was young. Later, illness, especially her father's deterioration, dampened their urge to fight. Her mother remained vigorous longer, picky and prickly. Rage diminished into midrange irritability, obsessive complaints about everything. When my patient was a child, her mother was given to self-absorbed, angry outbursts. Sex was associated with anger more than pleasure. Yet she noted that her parents talked more in bed than at any other time and that she felt comforted to hear their voices in the dark.

"My parents are in my leg, fighting and having sex. Mostly arguing. They've been there a long time. They should make me stronger, but I'm shaky. It's like having earthquakes in my leg. They're fighting to get out of their lives. To be free of each other, to be free of me. I'm holding them down, suffocating then. We're all claustrophobic. They loved me but felt stifled having a child."

She pictured her leg as phallic with vaginal insides, holding her parents, defusing them. limiting their threatening activity. Giving herself a leg to stand on. Holding them as she wished to be held. Filling herself without being filled. Not very satisfactory. A piece of dreamwork took advantage of a physical weakness to express a log jam of feelings. Her leg working overtime, doing too much psychic work, standing in for the psyche, symbolically overburdened, intermittently collapsing. Trying to put her psyche into too small a space, boundaries tight in the face of flooding, spilling, dread of the uncontainable.

"I don't think they touched me very much. I got along without being held. I pushed past being uncomfortable with myself, fighting off a need to cling. It's not exactly that I got used to it. I didn't know what I was missing. It's more that I learned to create a semblance of strength in danger of crumbling. But I got strong. I got through my breakdowns."

She was hospitalized three times between ages thirty and forty but has not been since. She pretty much saved herself, with a little psychiatric help. "I'm old now and my fears are coming back. They never really left, but my strength was stronger, my push was greater. I threw myself into the swim of things, and life carried me along. I succeeded in reducing life to workable modules. I fear falling apart as an old woman, not being able to take care of myself, deteriorating, resourceless. My friends are dying. There's no one to help me, a little like I felt as a child. I'm not sure I'm reaching out to you, but I'm here. It's some relief to share my life, but I wish I had someone close to share it with. Whatever was wrong with my parents, they talked to each other in bed."

Lust is associated with desire, desire with lack. If you have everything, there's no need to desire anything. Lust then, as a form of desire, is to want something you don't have.

God is imagined as being perfect. Does this mean God has no needs or lacks?

If God lacks desire, does this mean He is not absolute, since to be absolute means to lack nothing?

We ordinarily say that God desires us to desire Him. Desire as a positive. Not to desire is a lack. Desire itself as plenitude, a fullness, richness of life.

Clinically, people complain about lack of desire, lack of vitality, lack of self.

Lust for life. One envies those who have it.

In the *Upanishads*, Death offers many blessings to Nachiketas, not just all sweetness, earthly and heavenly, but the power to taste it. Without an ability to enjoy enjoyment, what is the latter? The same with lust. Lust is one thing, ability to be fulfilled through it another.

⟳ Lust as fullness. Lust as lack. What does it want? To possess the other? To have the other? To take the other? To satisfy itself on or with the other? To get great riches from the body of the other. We dig for riches in the richness of bodies.

⟳ When lust is mutual, lust meets lust. Lust adds to lust, fermenting, bubbling, boiling over, over and over. Desire unites with, rubs against, inflames desire. Desires mount, touch each other, breathe each other. A win-win situation. Flexing toward the maximum, beyond the maximum.

⟳ Lust as celebration, gift, grace, part of life's great bounty.

⟳ Yet we associate it with lack, with loss.

Split halves trying to make a whole. Plato's *Symposium*, the famous myth recounted by Aristophanes, of divided males and females, searching for the other half, whether male to male, female to female, female to male. Looking for soul mates, or simply mates.

Donald Hall describes sex with his wife, Jane, with her feet behind her head, fucking increasing fucking, or her legs twisted around his neck, acrobatics, suppleness, adding, adding to—to what? The feel of their lust, their amazingness, their dumbfoundedness, as if from body undoing body something transcendental is touched? Some unspoken, unseen transcendental acrobatics beyond sight and mind permeates the light that bodies grind into?

Such scenes from a book of tears, a cry issuing from his wife's death, a cry of loss. In the first parts of this book we hear about loss and the woman he loved. His poems take us on trips to her grave. After dwelling in grief, Hall takes us to their bed and tells us about their sex.

Hall speaks of this world, this earth, lust, love, loss as we know it here, this life. He does not mean anything transcendental, I added the transcendental. Ultimate loss (again I add too much, ultimate), to lose everything, he affirms, is fitting, delicious. This life, this loss, is enough, more than enough.

I gravitate to More. Some gravitate to Most. More is more than enough for me.

I'm not sure I've ever felt lust that didn't take me closer to God, open God for me.

Not everyone finds God through lust, but I don't think I'm merely an anomaly.

When you say this world, this life—whatever else can you mean? Where else do you experience the transcendental?

Lust fills me with God, with radiance. It is said we are sad after sex, there's a letdown, a loss. There's also a glow, an afterglow, with its own waves, feathers.

It is possible to feel guilty because of something in sex, but joy overtakes it.

Triumph can be part of it. What is this triumph? That we survived ourselves, survived nature, lived through upsurges? Once more the backcloth of destructiveness failed to win? That pleasure, orgasm, deliciousness, thrill, triumph over dread of disintegration? Sex did not kill us? We did not kill each other? That good feelings triumphed over bad feelings? That even in the face of bad feelings, the little good we feel is enough? Sometimes the good feeling peaks, and we are very happy. And when it subsides, we remember delicious goodness; it remains important. I feel the sum of good lusts in my life under my skin.

Triumph, too, is that we can indulge, fulfill, discover lust, once taboo. Withheld as a little child—so many years of fantasy. Finally, a partner. Stretching what bodies can do, what we feel through bodies. Again, again. Maybe it's what others do, only now it's us. Anxiety and guilt murmur, endless streams, but we do not stop.

An old man—a worker who has had a hard life—is dying. His wonderful daughter tells me he sent a dollar to every charity request he received. He was a rough man to be a daughter to. Now he is weak, in bed, masturbating in some fashion, his hand caressing his penis as if it were a woman (as it once caressed a woman, perhaps as if she were his penis). "I love you, I love you, oh, so sweet," passes his lips. His loneliness assuaged by a woman in his mind, in his skin, hovering over and under. He is breathless. Soothing himself, caring for himself, loving himself. He is *living*. His body, soul, heart an ineradicable yes.

Speculation: The triumph is of the body in the face of death, the body in death, as it is dying. Yes, of spirit too, self-feeling, life-feeling. All this in a body already disintegrating, sickly. Yes, it will die, Hamlet will hold its skull. The earth will be no more. But this moment, this feeling, this press toward orgasm, toward the home base of the other, will never die. It cannot die because it lives forever now.

Lust is always being evaluated. Either it is lower than something else on a scale of values or, if you don't have it, there's something wrong with you.

I believe in eternal life now. Not later. It's not a belief so much as a feeling. I suppose it must be true of pain, but I mainly feel it in joy, as Keats said of beauty ("A thing of beauty is a joy forever"). My most real lusts fuse with other moments, like the first time I heard Vivaldi or saw Kandinsky or saw the stars in heaven, summating into thanks and praise, akin to the delicately raucous, appreciative soul ache of the psalms.

A lot of people are more down to earth than I. I have a patient who wishes I showed more hate in sex. She feels murderously sexual, mean, bullying, submissive. She'll do anything I want. She wants to rim me. She wants me to do anything she wants. She'll fuck my ass wildly with her finger, her tongue, say cruel things. She'll jerk me off, blow me, drive me crazy. She feels I'm too squeaky clean, nice, and that she'd be guilty with me sexually. She is also beginning to feel gentle, something new. Her husband is not sure what's happening. They have to catch up to each other.

Is mutual rape possible? Isn't that a contradiction in terms? My patient tells me she wants us to rape each other. We *must* rape each other. Rape, indeed! With mutual consent. Is this *playing* at rape, the real thing? Surely, this is not what people mean by rape. This is something else, with rape in the background. In the foreground, something that looks like rape, simulates rape, *is* rape in spirit somehow, by implication, by laying on of hands, of organs. There is rape in the room, the smell of rape. *That* is necessary. My patient wants no less.

Green grape, no go.
Ripe grape, also no.
A bit of raisin?

Good man never gives up. Surely green and ripe would have been better. Is a bite of raisin better than nothing? A bit of raisin, at last? We know the answer. Here's one girl he doesn't get. One woman, one old lady who won't. Was wanting her enough? Not at all. Wouldn't having her be better? What *is* it the poet gets? Something, for sure—trickles of something.

Does one taste in not getting what one might have tasted if one got? I don't think so. But the poem is like a bite of grape; a taste of pleasure runs through it.

In the extreme case, not getting is a disease and makes one diseased. It's one thing to discover nothing as part of life. It's something else not to find life because there is nothing.

Some people remain alive after they starve to death. They go through life starved for living. Starvation is their emotional baseline. If something good comes their way, it is difficult to take in without getting sick. Emotional digestion needs a lot of exercise.

One feels the twinkle in the poet asking for a bit, a bite, a taste of raisin. Poets fuse pleasure with loss, nostalgia with wonder. A fish that got away turns into a poignant smile. One is, after all, speaking of time—our true love, original fickleness. slipperiness, shivers.

In Cavafy's poems, lust grows in loss. Lust streaked by loss, loss streaked by lust. This is so with special, if delicate, explicitness, as his work is set in the ancient past, in Greece, Alexandria, Syria, poems of antiquity. Loves, deaths, ambitions, hopes, despairs, tumult of flesh—gone long ago. All the more tantalizingly omnipresent, timeless, set so deeply in time.

A glimpse of chest, sudden tumescence, a pang—pulsations in memory. Memory set in a world in process of fading to itself: Constantinople, Alexandria, Damascus, Athens, Salamis, Rome, vanquished or on the verge of losing power and vitality, losing the life they knew. A life that still makes the poet proud. Pride of mind, flesh, spirit, fellow feeling—the human. Activities of man, lit up by art.

Some of the names we recognize, those of kings, heroes, teachers, gods. Others specialists may know. Some are chance finds, many imaginary. The situations are familiar as soon as we hear them. We know the strivings, the aloneness, the flaring up and collapse of longing and zest, the poignancy of connection and loss, the missed and achieved excitements. Somehow they seem more immediate because memory validates them.

Imaginative memory or simply imaginings—at some point it becomes irrelevant what is being remembered, what imagined. Memory and imagining drill through psyche and life. Psyche and life drill through us. Memory as a form of imagination, imagination permeated by memory. Feelings touch mouths on places no body can find.

Sensation through imagined memory. One doesn't ask what is real, what imagined. It is all real, all imagined. Cavafy speaks of the return of sensation "when the lips and the skin remember, / and the hands feel as if they touch again." Sensation long gone lights the present; memory and imagining replenish each other. It may even be that the sensation he remembers never happened except as imagining. His work is filled with made-up scenes, imaginary sensation. Yet quickening, awakening. Sensation remembered, imagined, or both brings one to life.

Or is it imagination that brings one to life?

Was the original sensation as good as the remembered or fabricated one? Better? Of course, better. Young immersion in what body can feel, covered by fantasy, breathing the real. Remember?

Fanned to life by a poem or created by a poem. The poem reaches a place sensation presses toward but does not quite find by itself. Sensation is its own fulfillment, certainly. But it needs poetry to complete it, to sing its ringing incompletion. Sensation is raw, naked without a poem.

We are not speaking of competition between then and now, sensation and image. We are noting that deep in the well of the poem, immersed in time, we see what life can do when it meets itself. Is it possible that the dimming of time can make sensation more intense, more valuable? Time passing makes time shine.

In another poem, Cavafy creates a scene he places twenty-six years earlier, a bar in the heat of summer, "Enjoyment of the flesh between / our half-opened clothes; / quick baring of the flesh," excitement unable to wait, a vision of flashing bodies coming to rest in the poem. Was the older man from ancient Greece or Rome, remembering his youth, waiting to bring his youth alive over a thousand years later, created in a poem by a feeling man in the twentieth century, stirring us now?

Another, more placid moment, outside a house of pleasure the man knew in his youth, he stands and looks at the door, lingering, gazing, "my whole being radiating the sensual emotion stored up inside." Inside the body, the flesh, the mind, the heart, the poem. Not inside a bar, not grazing with a partner unable to wait many years ago. Now waiting is what happens. Waiting through the years. And inside the waiting, radiance.

Sensation is part of the life of the poem. But the poem does not simply light up sensation or become lit by it. Nor does it merely memorialize sensation or frame it, a signet stamp in words. The poem becomes part of life quivering, like a drop of water catching the light. We may feel a bit sad, a bit happy, taste pleasure, passage, the beginning and the end, feel living is worthwhile as we disappear, a slight smile of wonder, of caring for what life gives us, the poetry that runs through it. We wonder for ourselves, what can it mean that we are poetic beings, tutored by sensation? Imaginative bodies? Even holiness, like eros, requires fancy.

Cavafy (the poet, narrator, voice of the poem) says to lose oneself in erotic sensation is a necessary precondition for a life of poetry. What he doesn't quite say, but his whole work says: poetry that honors sensation brings the most out of what the latter offers. Poetry, more than other forms of human expression, speaks to unities of sensa-tion/symbol/real, probing and sharing turns of this astonishing gift.

What is honored, tasted, gifted through Cavafy's poetry are shiv-ers of life that might have been, almosts and maybes, as well as direct hits and fuelings. Deliciousness of what didn't happen:

> Body, remember not only how much you were loved,
> not only the beds you lay on,
> but also those desires that glowed openly
> in eyes that looked at you,
> trembled for you in the voices . . .

All that happens when we see each other. Hidden and not so hid-den tremolos, the glow, always the glow. Beings that glow—what could be better? Radiant shivers. Where are these shivers? Under and over and through the skin? Tantalizing swirls in the underside of body? Feelings that tremble in voices? What about *that* unity, that commonality of the human species—*one* in *trembling*?

> After a taste of Cavafy, how crude of me to say what it's like to ride the subway on the way to work in New York City. But there you have it. So many stony faces, stiff bodies, punctuated with smiles, twinkles, flickers of stars through haze. Now and then you get coarse acts, a man rubbing on someone. But I see all kinds of things in women's faces, in their bodies, as they see in mine. A lot of quivering inside stone.

I don't think I've ever come on the subway. But I might have. I doubt it could happen now that I'm older. But it could.

So much sex on the way to work. I can't count all the fucking. So many women have this or that good thing that arrests interest, tends toward arousal.

I've discovered forms of sex I didn't know existed. Skin to skin contact while three to ten feet apart. I feel a woman's cheek or lips or forehead in or on mine and distance matters, because the feel is not the same near or far, so many gradations of nearer, farther. In the spring and summer it is easy to feel arm to arm contact fifteen feet away. You'd think this kind of touch would be harder in the winter, covered with long-sleeve shirts, sweaters, vests, coats. But no, we feel it. Arms feel it. And we feel our arms turn into tendrils or funnels sucking quivers from body to body, up the arm, down the chest toward home, from home to toes. While other streams go up the back, the back of the head, sides of the head, and foreheads where there are fevers in illness and fevers in health. Try pretending it's the chill of the cold, but that is silly. We do know what is going on. We know through and through.

And all this starts with seeing?

That's on the subway. I haven't said a word about the block between the subway stop and work. Once you're out in Manhattan (I ride from Brooklyn) everything changes. Women are thinner, brighter, better dressed (not necessarily more sensuous). More beauty on one block in half a minute than on a half-hour walk in Brooklyn. One punch in the gut after another. I may never walk the block. I feel like I'm on an escalator going the other way, carried backward by the kick of the shots. The world is going backward, backward, one luminous vision after another.

I have experimented. Opening to every single woman I go by. *Every* one. Homely, ugly, plain, business faces, fuzzy faces, sensuous skin, tight skin—*all*! The hits are different, some thud, clang, some sing on key or off. The tuning fork rings some way with everyone.

By the time I get to my office, I've had a full day. It feels like I've lived through many full days. And soon, my women patients come.

Lacan has some outrageous notions that add colorful skeins to the background tapestry of lust. It is not unusual to associate lust with death, and Lacan gives this link a tweak. He begins with a little pseudo-biology, as Freud does with life and death drives. Lacan speaks of a lamella as amoeba-like, motile, able to survive division, in some sense immortal, an organ "whose characteristic is not to exist"—a kind of conceptual, mythic reference to libido. He relates the lamella and libido "to what the sexed being loses in sexuality."

Immediately, a Gnostic ring. In Gnostic vision, the soul in heaven must be induced, seduced to enter a moist womb-being on the way to earthly birth. To partake in earthly development is a fall from pristine immortality. A sense of loss is attached to becoming an embodied being. A sense of loss aggravated throughout life.

Lacan's twist is to make libido immortal prior to sexed reproduction. He performs an abstraction on the sense of life and conceptually propels a result into a philosophical psychoanalytic forever. "It is the libido, *qua* pure life instinct, that is to say, immortal life, that has need of no organ, simplified indestructible life. It is precisely what is subtracted from the living being by virtue of the fact that it is subject to the cycle of sexed reproduction."

An astonishing statement, yet with a wide background. Human beings have long performed this kind of reduction in their own ways, that is, distilling the sense of life out of the matrix of experience. We can try to focus attention on pure life-feeling. Where is our sense of aliveness? Is it more one place or another at different times, spreading, gathering more in this or that organ, skin, invisible insides of body? Is it nowhere? Do we distill it out of our bodies as an object of imaginative reflection? Locate it in an imaginary point with blurry edges? Is it in breath, in blood, in various energy centers, in vision, in impalpable intuition?

It is difficult to pin down what status the concept of life has in Lacan's work. A priori structure, structural condition of psyche, fetching myth, whacko idea? Libido as silly putty, fun to play with. Not the Jungian notion of general psychic energy. Not exactly a Freudian read of sexuality. Libido as pure life instinct, essence, distilled. Postulating simplified, immortal, indestructible, irrepressible life, with no need of organ, is a little like Galileo postulating a pure vacuum. Something that does not or cannot exist illuminates existence.

The focus is life as such, not subject to reproduction, not subject to existing organs. Lacan calls it an organ that does not exist, an "ungraspable organ," "false organ." A true organ would be genitals, systems mediating hormonal chemistry, skin, something concretely physical. But the idea of life itself, subtracted from the matrix of living experience, is a signifier, part of the life of meaning found nowhere.

There are different ways to take Lacan's thinking, and I'll move in and out of a few of them, taking liberties. First, life as signifier (life, libido, Lacan slides between them). Plenitude, fullness, pulse, drive. Pure, immortal life—nothing seems to be missing.

He playfully likens life going on forever to a lamella, which he links to an omelet, which in French has reference to man (*homme-lette*), the life of man. Not a homunculus, not the little man inside the brain. He imagines something flying off in birth, something to do with membranes (or eggs) breaking. Meaning as membrane breaking, flying off.

Life is not only life. It *means* life. As a signifier, it means everything life can mean. It remains open, ready for more. Lacan's image of birth is not accidental. Birth of meaning, meaning in incessant birth. Children are born one or two at a time. Meanings pour out, proliferate, fly off every which way in tumult. Meanings pile on and mix, like an imaginary omelet in which ingredients grow as it cooks. If life did not *mean* life to us, we would not be making so big a deal about it. It is precisely because life is an open signifier that we cannot stop filling it. The tantalizing, leading-you-on quality built into life is exacerbated, accelerated, by creation of meaning.

"Lamella" literally means thin scale, membrane, plate, layer of tissue or bone. On the internet I found a site of beautiful lamella radiating images, possibly taking off from leaflike structures on the underside of mushrooms. Lacan associates lamella with amoebas, life dividing without sexed reproduction. He reaches for a sense of livingness without death. Pure living tissue, perhaps, or membrane or X that goes on and on. Nothing lives forever (funny phrase—Nothing as undying life). Lamella, amoeba—as if anything biological can be deathless. Lacan uses these images as jolts, not simply as literal realities, catapulting us to entertain what it means when death is more elusive than life.

That a biological entity lives without end is unreal, and Lacan takes us on a trip to the unreal. The unreal is very real for us in a host of ways. We say he, she, or it is unreal when we mean far out, cool, amazing. We may also mean something very painful—when feeling unreal is agonizing. Then again, a sense of the unreal clings to experiencing, part of the way life feels. Various enlightenment pursuits are concerned with waking up, becoming real. Individuals speak of cutting through the veil of unreality, the caul, the bell jar. A degree of depersonalization seems to be part of distance, reflection, thinking, consciousness.

We associate unreality, too, with madness, which involves damage to common sense reality. And if Lacan calls libido an unreal organ, we will not be surprised to discover meldings of libido and madness. Lacan's unreal, like so much else in his work, is elusive. It functions something like a philosophic idea, or a postulate, a little like an unreal or imaginary number. Or a unicorn. Or something as mythic as Freud's "witch," his metapsychology. The unreal has one foot in lived reality (when we feel unreal, experience something as unreal), another in concept formation (the unreal as structure of unconscious functioning). We will leave open, for the moment, where other feet are.

"The libido is the essential organ in understanding the nature of the drive. The organ is unreal. Unreal is not imaginary. The unreal is defined by articulating itself on the real in a way that eludes us, and it is precisely this that requires that its representation should be mythical, as I have made it. But the fact that it is unreal does not prevent an organ from embodying itself."

Unreal, deathless life, is a poetic real, a mad real. Very real unreal, very unreal real. A mythic life, a life that drives us, unreal organ of the real. That unreality limns reality may be a poetic realization but testifies to a structure of the real for us. To divest reality of unreality is an act of murder. To take the unreal out of the real is, at least, a castration of the real. The very fullness of life is partly mythic.

It is, of course, delusional to restrict the plenitude of life to deathlessness. There may be a deathless aspect to the sense of plenitude, or to the structure of plenitude. Lacan posits deathless life in its irrepressible fullness as a dramatic foil to loss that plunges toward death, anticipates and contains hints of death. Irrepressibly deathless life is unreal but clings as a penumbra to real life. The unreal, then, is part of the structure of the real, as much as loss or death is.

Lacan is on the scent of pristine or originary or primal loss. Loss is built into the structure of time, past-present-future commingling, more than co-reciprocal. Loss is part of plenitude, plenitude part of loss. Lacan's audacious move is to posit primal loss as loss of deathless libido, crossing from life as such to sexed reproduction, consequently death. Other losses partake of this primal structure, this crossover. Dialectics of loss and fullness draw on sexed existence "replacing," taking over and substituting for mythic fullness, life without end, life at its maximum now and forever.

The panoply of loss and wound charted by psychoanalysis—birth, weaning, separation, castration anxieties, leaving one world for another all through life, loss and gain together—all tap unconscious mythical repletion of immortal life and the fall into fecundity and death. We hear biblical echoes in Lacan's chant, although fall, loss, lack is not simply contingent on disobedience but the structure of things (disobedience itself exhibits a gain/loss structure).

Lust attempts to make the unreal real. It reaches immortal life, life at its fullest, its maximum, as if a maximum goes on forever. A taste of immortality, consummation that will never end. Never-ending consummation becomes a background drive, an order, a command, a desire. An impossibility. With one lust or another, one tries to make the impossible possible, to hold the unreal through the real. It cannot be done, of course, not fully. But one dips in, gets tastes.

Immortality surrounds temporality. Temporality ruptures immortality, but the latter as unconscious background tries to fill the gaps in time. Lacan, like Freud, had notions of unconscious timelessness and deathlessness, an unreal that glistens in the real. Lust straddles both worlds. It peaks in time, taps into eternity. Pleasurable, orgasmic sensations, temporal pulsations, for the moment going on forever. Part of the sadness of loss, from ancient times on, fuses loss of immortality with loss of bodily fluids. One reason lust sometimes spends itself by satisfaction is the realization, afterward, that one's bid for immortality failed. One can't keep oneself or the other filled with time or timelessness. Nevertheless, the capacity to fuse time with timelessness in passing acts of sex, heightened by lust, amazes consciousness and provides endless food for thought. Exciting moments and time to sort things out, medleys of gains and losses.

Sparrow was in a love-hate relationship with her father and love-hate relationships with men. Her father was sexy, successful, vigorous, virile. Her mother was semihysterically meticulous about her body, its beauty, its aches and pains. She would have lost herself in body as signifier of sex and status and the temptation of chronic plastic surgery, but the outer body of home saved her. Obsession with decorating her homes (one in the city, two in the country) was the other side of caring for body, but external focus extended her horizons. By the time her children were out of the house, she was in business as a consultant, decorating the homes of others. As confidence grew, need for doctors lessened.

Sparrow spent a lot of time in childhood taking care of her mother and fighting arousal by her father. He saw her as his bathing beauty, model, sex star of the future, father's darling now. He was distant as a person, absorbed in business and financial cares, a good dresser, who smelled good, and Sparrow admired him. It was not until her teens that she could articulate the difference between the strong feeling she got from him and the fact that he did not know her emotionally—did not, could not, as he lacked capacity for finding her as a person. He knew her as body, as image. When she looked good, he smiled and said nice things. When she looked bad, he was critical, turned off. To get an affect charge from him she had to be attractive.

As she grew, she developed sympathy for her mother's plight but could not bear the latter's hypochondriacal concerns. To be obsessed with the small world of body—Sparrow recoiled at such constriction. Flying was an important image for her. Stretching wings. She filled her walls with pictures she painted of birds. Flying from home, from body. She felt soul, spirit—or wanted to.

In college she became a meditator, did yoga, studied Buddhism. After college she added acupuncture, chiropractory, dance classes, mime, and in her thirties, Kabbalah. She had a series of different kinds of therapies, including work designed to expand her brain's capacity to process complex input. She never tried psychoanalysis—it was nixed in her milieu. Someone in Kabbalah seminar brought my work up and piqued her interest. She began to read, and saw herself in some of my cases.

My work on catastrophe and faith fit what she was learning in Kabbalah. Trauma maims and kills but also ignites inspired living. She felt her trauma was not so much what happened to her as what didn't. Perhaps too much emphasis on the physical, not enough on the personal. Sparrow wanted to live an inspired life and her flame had moments, but something dampened it and went wrong. It peaked and fell flat, over and over.

Her childhood was rich with people, parents' friends and their children, business friends, her own friends. There was not much alone time. People were not really close to each other but there were strong feelings, loud voices. As a child it struck her, although she could not put it into words, that her parents and their friends talked *at* rather than to or with each other. They took turns monologing. One recited stories and things that happened to him or her, then another did. There were no real interchanges so far as Sparrow could see, no chance for mutual transformation. Later in life, Sparrow realized that exchange of feelings can go on invisibly beneath the surface, and that a lot of impact and response might have taken place outside awareness.

Some people lit her up, some made her feel sorry for them, some made her want to run away and hide. She got used to feeling lots of things with lots of personalities. It's not that she was deprived of feelings. She was known and seen and appreciated. Except that the acknowledgment she received was not specific to her. It was part of the noisy camaraderie that graced the air she breathed. Lots of noisy affect, much of it positive, but not particularly meaningful. A high-carb emotional diet. *Who* was smiled at, patted on the back, made much of? A fine person we called, The Acknowledged Sparrow, a bubbly, generic little girl. But there was someone important inside, someone she didn't quite know, someone very close, intimate, invisible, quiet. Someone inside the noise. All her life she sensed mystery no one talked about. Everyone lived in it under the bonhomie of daily bustle.

She started going from one male to another at a very young age. By fourteen, male-hopping was an established pattern. Organized defiance made her proud. But it also bothered her and in her twenties bothered her a lot. She had no defenses against it. It was something she did. Lust surfboarding. Pleasure blurred a sense of dislocation, the latter mounting as years passed.

She loved the feeling of attraction, of seeing a man light up when he looked at her. A man in the middle of doing something, looking at her, caught like a deer by headlights. A rise of feeling, body warming all over, climbing, trying to get out. Many men, happy feelings, then flat, dying suddenly. Lifting up, dying out. Even when she hoped a relationship would last, her or her partner's feelings abruptly changed.

She knew this had to do with her father, with her mother. It had to do with his valuing her attractiveness, turning on and off depending how on she looked. What did he see? Skin, curves, features. For moments, in his eyes, her body was more intact, healthy, exquisite than her mother's. Through his look, her body achieved a vital wholeness, but when the look faded, crumbling started. One man after another put her body back together, but, like Humpty-Dumpty, she found that wholeness didn't last. Sparrow's beauty grew around a sense of emotional blindness that made her suffer as she got older.

She tried to compensate through spiritual awareness, a quiet sense of self within, unacknowledged, indefinite, not quite seen or heard. But self in stillness didn't stand a chance when a male face lit up at the sight of her.

Sparrow came to realize she was a kind of addict: (1) addicted to high doses of emotion without specific nutrients, followed by painful crashes; (2) addicted to high doses of pleasure in place of emotional digestion; (3) addicted to painful crashes.

Nevertheless, learning went on in bursts of lust. Attraction was not merely blind. Sparrow wanted to fly, but learning came through her body. Her whole body was a kind of cognitive organ, lust an important teacher. Some people learn by using their heads; Sparrow learned by losing hers. Sexual enactment was a form of tasting and sifting. Sex has a taste, and men taste differently. Each brings different parts of life, different dangers. She used her body the way a baby uses its tongue: to test, to evaluate, to decide whether to take in or spit out. As if sexuality took the place of emotional digestion.

In our five years together, Sparrow's cycling with men slowed down. She began listening to what her body was telling her. Her body conveyed a lot of information about men she was close to, but Sparrow flew over it. Her body brimmed with ignored messages. Therapy gave her time to listen. It was less a matter of head learning than paying attention to body cues. Her body's warnings went unheeded. Her body would point Sparrow toward or away from one man or another, even announced what it thought she would or could not get from one or the other. But she missed messages or could not act on them in the din of arousal.

In therapy, she began to distinguish between kinds of arousal, kinds of drops. Words never were the most important thing for Sparrow, but they played a role. Our meetings gave her a chance to let words spin into body words, to talk about what body was feeling, running subtitles to mute excitement. It was not a matter of control from the top, but finding direction from body sensing, to access the feel of what was there.

An important finding was that Sparrow hated bypassing herself but felt in despair of acting on anything she might learn if she paid attention. Her patterns possessed her and she was helpless against them. She didn't listen to herself because she didn't think there was much she could do. She was used to arousal drowning her out. Our meetings gave her a chance to touch herself and say that she hated something about the way her life felt. The incessant rush to aliveness, fall into death, constant oscillation between excitement and crash. She was angry at the pattern of her life. It no longer stood her well. It was not getting anywhere and she was getting older. We were working two years, she was thirty-six, when the aching words came out of her: "I want to have a baby. I want the baby to have a father." A longing spinning into words. She seared herself with words, and words came alive.

How would motherhood come about, given Sparrow's track record? Very little in her adult life indicated she would find pleasure in, have ability for, or endure co-creating a family.

"Things aren't right, and I've had enough. For years I felt my life taking the wrong turn. It was all right when I was younger, but something never righted itself. Spinning wheels, sex everywhere, missing a feeling center. I did not want to feel how wrong things were. I wanted everything to be OK. Inside lust was a baby wanting to be born. I knew it. I felt it. There was nothing to do about it. At least I had pleasure. At some point I heard babies inside the pleasure but shut them out. I didn't just have orgasms, I felt babies. Orgasm babies that were never born. That will never be born. I'm afraid I'll miss what's important. When I die, my stone will say, 'She had fun—no love.' Excitement and pain but no one to care for, no one who cares."

Where was this caring family to come from?

There are times when you see how God created the universe out of nothing. You see it because it happens now.

Sparrow left me after five years work when she was pregnant. She was living with a teacher younger than herself, whom she met at the school they taught in. They had a rocky relationship, repeatedly breaking up and getting back together. Little by little, it stabilized. Fights in place of breakups, arguments in place of fights, bickering in place of arguments. A process in motion. Would the stormy atmosphere subside by the time the baby was born? Would there be good enough weather in time for a child not to be scarred too badly? I heard about Sparrow some years later from a friend she gave my number to. Sparrow was a mother of two, contemplating going back to work, part of a family very much in progress. I don't know many details.

Going through this on the therapist's side is a kind of gestation and birth. How does it happen? I don't have answers, but I'll share some threads. Therapy gives some people a place to feel themselves and their lives without being rushed out of them. "This is what it's like to be me. This is what it's like to feel alive." So often, someone tries to talk us out of it or we brush ourselves off. With all the exposure to good things—therapies, creative classes, meditation—it's difficult to understand how Sparrow failed to get the feel of her life or link up with it for so long a time. On the other hand, in her mid-thirties is not so long, after all—perhaps for her it was just right. Perhaps it took that long for her discontent to pick up enough momentum for the sort of work I do to be useful. I think I gave her permission to feel bothered by herself just as she was getting ready to feel how bothered she was.

And what about the therapeutic, creative, spiritual, and sexual riches that crisscrossed her life through her twenties and the first half of her thirties? After much reflection, my conjecture is that the activities that led to these, in some important way, reinforced her immortality. They nourished her and helped her grow in a way suggested in the preceding section: they affirmed her life-feeling at the expense of her life. They revved up her sense of being alive, her sexuality, creativeness, spirituality, without regarding her personal timeline, the overall course of her life. Heightened experiences of the moment pushed past the ache within. The ache within was contacted as something to use creatively, something to explore and transcend, not to be listened to or dwelled with in its own right. The ache of living did not get its due. Irrepressible life, pure life-feeling was enhanced at the expense of the particular person living it.

I do not want to play down what these activities did for Sparrow, not just helping her to get through, but adding to the fullness of, existence. They are part of her, tools to draw on for the rest of her life. Perhaps all the things she did helped to prepare her to meet herself in ways postponed. Focusing on riches blot out poverty. Sparrow built herself up until she could face what was wrong, the dreaded disabled and impoverished areas of self.

It sounds odd to say sex was used in the service of immortality. What is more time bound than lust? But following the life drive, the irrepressible surge, blotted out Sparrow's full existence. It gave her terrific experiences but only an aspect of herself. Lust enabled her to enjoy intensity without dealing with difficult feelings. Things began and ended with a bang. A flight and a crash, a pattern that permeated her life. She went from job to job, interest to interest, as well as man to man.

There are conflicts in the body, for example, clashes between pleasure and fecundity. We are lucky when capacities work together. Often they rub against each other, an uncomfortable friction difficult to sustain. Sensing tensions of our nature, dipping in, getting the feel of inherent conflict can makes us more able, more resonant. We do not need solutions in order to grow.

Sparrow sensed she was in danger, but partners, classes, spiritual activities failed to confirm her worry. They encouraged what was good in her life, got her past drops. That her life involved one change of direction after another was applauded as a strong life. Others looked at the plus side while she treaded water. Her aliveness, her sparkle muted concern about her distress, made it difficult for others to fully take in her distress. It felt good being near her.

"I'm lusting my life away," she complained. "Following my bliss, my good feeling. Like crumbs in the forest, men, classes, jobs. Where are these crumbs leading me? My life eats them and they're gone. Something remains, yes, but is anything building? I once thought they were diamonds, gems of experience. Now I want more, something else."

It is hard for me to believe that I am the first person in her life who listened and believed how badly she felt. Perhaps a difference is I listened and kept listening, and her care registered. That it registered with me gave her a chance to link up with it. Perhaps the pleasure, glow, attractiveness, the good feeling that emanated from her body threw others off track. Threw her off as well. It is to her credit that she stuck with it, and stuck with it some more. She broke through the irrepressible immortality of the life-feeling to produce and live life.

Therapy's contribution is modest but genuine, giving the ache of life a chance to be heard. Lust was an important part of Sparrow's tenacity. Yet I think lust was lonely, wanting a place in a fuller psychic reality, a larger feeling self. Given a chance, psychic sensing (there was an itch, a rub where it was lacking or not responded to) developed enough to connect with what her body self was going through, what her life was asking.

Lust gets us into families. Lust gets us out.

Jeri tells me she's not interested in writing. She used to write for women's magazines before becoming a therapist. "Sometimes I still sit down to try. What comes out are clichés, trivia, girly things like I used to do. My writing hasn't changed since I was a teen. It's not something you want to keep doing if that's the way it is."

My papers had just started coming out in journals. I was upgraded in her eyes and toyed with making a move. Jeri felt good to be with. She was attractive, bright, active, a ball of energy. Too made-up for my taste, but I appreciated her wish to attract. I felt a little rise when she was near. I wondered what sex would be like and thought, well why not a few times anyway?

I couldn't quite push myself past a barrier. Fear, worry, inhibitions? A piece of lust was missing. Was it her face, her expression? Something tight, brittle? Her voice, a subtly loud twang in it?

My mind goes its own way, put-downish in this case: "She's too materialistic. Into her cool apartment, clothes, made-up face. Too made-up. Too Lord and Taylor." I could not push past the mask.

"Listen," my counter-mind would say, "she's a good gal, a nice gal. She's been good to you. She's good to people. She affirms. She's not into cosmic struggle. She's not dedicated to inner torment. She wants to feel good, have a good time. What's wrong with you!"

We might have come close a couple of times, but a force of repulsion intervened. We never made it, never really tried. We liked speaking to each other from time to time, and I heard about Brinkly, the most important of her loves (if "love" is the right word).

At the time, I could not stand Brinkly. He didn't have a therapy soul. Jeri didn't either. They were competent, efficient, did their jobs, but didn't eat and sleep them. The sense that therapy was a spiritual calling, a form of prayer couldn't be farther from their minds. For them, therapy was a business, a decent way to make a living, helpful, benevolent, but not consuming, not transforming.

Gradually, it dawned on me that Jeri and Brinkly were an item, although he was married. The affair lasted several years. When she saw that I suspected, she told me all about it. "What a beautiful man, a beautiful body. I feel what I've always wanted to feel." Sex was wonderful. Touch was heaven. Feeling each other sublime. Lust totally fulfilled and fulfilling. A dream come true.

That they would never live together suited Jeri fine, so she said. It's not that she loved aloneness. She treasured the time she and Brinkly were together. But she knew she was not the kind of person to share a life for long. She was in her forties. Moments of heightened beauty and pleasure were enough. Rather, she liked the feeling that she couldn't get enough of them. Extended moments, now and then, a little more.

I lost contact with Jeri and seven years later heard she had died. I felt badly and wanted to know the details, but my warped mind included in its panegyrics moralistic pronouncements like, "Live by the body, die by the body." A warped superego never dies.

I knew many people who died young. My little brother's death just before his eleventh birthday was not because of lust. "The wages of sin is death." I went to West Street, stared a long time into the black waters of the Hudson River, jumped in and drowned.

Did I ever have as full a sexual experience as Jeri?

I certainly tried my best. At times I almost did. Maybe I did and didn't know. Maybe I imagined I did. Always something holding back. Isn't that the point? Isn't that what is meant by fucking out of my mind? Fucking your brains out? Is it the heart that goes past the mind? Can the body alone do it?

"I tolerate guilt better. Not that I'm happy with the way things are. But I'm doing the best I can. That's a new feeling, I think true.

"My girlfriend calls me her sweetie. I never had this before. Last night I went over after eleven. She takes a shower, tells me to come in, sucks me off in the shower. While we dry she bends over her desk and we fuck. It's pure sensation. Pure sensation, what a phrase. Why do we call sensation pure? We put sensation down, think it less than thinking, feel it less than feeling. I feel lucky tasting pure sensation.

"I fucked a lot when I was young and was hot for my wife when we met. I was hot for her for years. It wore out with marital war. Having children did sex in. My wife put herself into bringing them up. Things got worse in slow increments. You think it's not happening, it's temporary, lust will come back. It gets worn away with arguments, chores, fatigue. Fighting over who's right when things go wrong with the kids. Everything irritates. An immune response sets in. We blot each other out to survive."

Sex between Kyle and his wife came and went for years. They had good moments in a sea of arguments and accusations, which gradually became a baseline mood. Kyle believed things worsened because his wife was not working outside the home. She put on weight, lost interest in anything other than the kids. He thought women who worked took better care of themselves. She did not want to miss being a full-time mother. He partly blamed her for his not being a better father. If she worked, he could work less and spend more time at home. He loved the kids. He convinced himself he wanted to spend more time with them, felt he *should*, and would have if he weren't the only breadwinner. Most families he knew had two incomes. He did not like to admit the arrangement suited him, that he liked being out of the house. It opened possibilities. It took years for him to realize how conflicted he was: wanting to be in *and* out of the house.

He barely guessed how angry he was that his wife won the battle of the home. She was getting something he couldn't give to himself. He couldn't afford to and didn't really want to. But he did want to be more of a father. He saw the difference it made when he spent more time at home. *She* may have gotten narrower. But *she* has her women friends, other mothers who get together with children, playgrounds, lunches, phone calls. He had work and his girlfriend. The nourishment his wife got through immersion in the children's daily life was something he tasted intermittently. He knew he was missing out, knew he wanted more but knew he didn't want as much of it as she did.

He seriously wondered if his wife *ever* lusted after him. *He* was attracted to *her* when they were young and couldn't get enough of her for years. She was acquiescent, enjoyed him, but he could count on one hand the times she had initiated sex. He could think of only two or three times when excitement drove her toward him—two or three times in two or three decades. His "sweetie" jumps him two or three times a night. *She* can't get enough of *him*. He does not remember *ever* being more appreciated by a woman.

"What is love?" he asks. "I made a romantic choice when I was young that wore out over the years. Would I marry my wife now? I doubt it. I'd want someone who could interact, not just blame and defend. Someone with active interests, more able to share. All the women I know do things outside the home. She's the only one stuck in it. She never takes a shred of responsibility for anything that goes wrong between us. Whatever it is, it's my fault. She shields herself from blame with discontent and resentment. Thinks it's up to me to make it up to her. To make up for what she never got and didn't become.

"I've begun to see sense in arranged marriages. Maybe they're not so bad. You don't begin with love. romance, the illusion of connection. You have to build connection. You start knowing relationship takes work. You have to learn to be together, do your share, contribute. You don't start with swimming eyes lost in lust. A thrill filled me when I saw my wife. What was I thinking?

"Do I love my girlfriend? Maybe I just appreciate being appreciated. Would I marry her? I don't think so, and I'm not sure she'd want that. What we have is about all she can handle. She likes seeing me a few times a week and having time for herself. There's not enough between us for a marriage. It's fun being with her. More than fun. but we don't have much in common. She has her life, I have mine. Would we like it if we had to live together? It's good in small doses.

"I was talking about guilt. My kids called my cell phone. Asked if I'd be home early. They wanted to show me things they did. I told them I had to work late. This happens a lot. A few years ago I might have sped home to eat with them. More often than not, it ended with fights over dinner, going to bed crying. When I'm away, good feelings build. I forget what it's like in reality. Last night I took the guilt and was rewarded by my girlfriend. She was grateful and showed it.

"It's not just 'hedonistic'—a word putting down aliveness of life. And it's not just dirty, illicit. It's transcendent. A naughty treat, like ice cream. The best sex. A taste of the goodness of life.

"I don't know if it's good for my marriage. I've no answer and keep going, sustaining the guilty tension. I've felt guilty all my life. I'm getting better at tolerating it. I've been a good boy, a responsible boy, and it's not good to be *too* good. I've been trying to find a healthy space for a little sociopathy. I'm a little proud of not being too good. I'm learning to face down my guilt, but I don't want to be immoral. I do want to be a good parent and spouse. I don't want to hurt anyone really."

"I've got the biggest dick in the world. Want to see it?" Lee was a mess, just out of the hospital, on heavy doses of antipsychotic meds. His wife brought him to see me, stays with him. He goes to open his pants and she stops him. "Behave for the doctor," she says. She looks at me funny, communicating he's like this, what can we do?

He talks about making girls bleed and how they love it. They cry out in pain for more. They can't get enough of him, of *it*. His wife holds one of his hands; the other gesticulates, paints pictures.

He tells me the nurses took peeks, and one sucked him. He fucked another in the med dispensary. I know the hospital he came out of. None of this is likely. None of it impossible. My mind wavers, not sure what's real. As soon as that happens, I take it as a signal. He makes me feel his dilemma, uncertainty about what's real, uncertainty about reality. He heads for his dick. Only his cock is real. *It must* be real. But his ideas about it are unreal. A ghastly, awesome predicament. Trying to nail the world to his cock. "I fuck, therefore I am." You almost think this will work. I remember kids in school showing hard-ons in their pants, searching for awe. Lee might have been one of them.

"Awesome dick," he whimpers angrily, a pleading, defiant cry.

His wife bends over and whispers, "You know he doesn't do too well. He needs Viagra. He comes fast and stays soft."

His favorite sexual act is lap dancing. He goes to bars and watches girls undress and burn his cock in his pants with their ass. His wife sits next to him, holds his hand. They come and go together.

What sort of therapy will we have? I look inside his head and see girls on his lap, girls dancing in his head. I'm frightened when I see the girls turn into snakes. His head filled with snakes. It will take a long time to unravel them.

Bernadette came anywhere, everywhere—a man's touch, the touch of the wind, her thoughts could set her off. Orgasm was cellular. She came in therapy when she shared fantasies. She was sensitive all over. One of her first statements was an understatement: "I come easily," she said at the beginning of our first session.

A very attractive woman. When she was younger, responsiveness held her together. Touch was like taste. Being with a man made her whole. The feel of skin brought her to tears, made heart smile. Every touch a teat. To come together with every breath. Full.

She does not know when fucking started to disorganize her. She pins it on nights with a man who never stopped. He had incessant orgasms fucking, fucking, fucking night after night. The next thing she knew she was hospitalized. He broke her down. Fucking broke her open, broke her down.

She was scattered sperm climbing into her eggs, staying there, hiding in her womb, swallowing her body, an unattached baby, an embryo not yet formed, fucking formlessness. She swayed inside and never came out, always about to form, never doing it. In the hospital she took up yoga and little by little began a process of recovery. Sitting still let the womb go back inside, and she had an outside again.

Once outside, she discovered Tantric yoga. A shared womb, slow, still sex without coming. No orgasm. Stillness quietly building. Just plain sex, the thing that once held her together, shattered. Slowly, she grew around the shatter. A single, sweeping coming, rising from below, from underneath her sitting, softness through her insides, encompassing her. She speaks of feeling/seeing golden orbs, liquids pulsing, again sliding into orgasm, in slow waves. It came from someplace below her body, under everything that could be found, breathing sweetness into her. Her body survives neither whole nor shattered. She did not have to be hospitalized again.

Lily was chronically raped by close relatives before she found her way into an American family after the Vietnam War. She blossomed. As a teen, she was and felt "juicy." She liked sex with guys she didn't know. She was highly charged and very bright. She became a literature major in college, attracted to portrayals of the human condition. Then something clicked off. Literature began to be a meaningless exercise, a dumb puppet show. She studied math, then business administration, and graduated with a triple major. After college she experimented with jobs and then began a software company, cresting with the computer industry to become a multimillionaire.

She drifted from man to man. The first "hit" was best, night with a stranger. A fling with the unknown, like throwing herself into space with no points of orientation. Once she knew a guy it was over. Her feelings turned off. She connected turning off with potential closeness, associated with childhood abuse by men close to her. The insight was clear but didn't help much.

Her twenties were exciting, as she was moving ahead at work and having terrific experiences with men. When she got the idea of staying longer with a man, she hit a limit. Whenever a conflict arose between lust for newness and building a relationship, the former won hands down. It took years for a wish for relationship to create real disturbance.

Lily met Arnie the night after an orgy. She had taken to group sex and was coasting along, expecting Arnie to be a little fling. She liked a lot of men around her, lots of stimulation. One-on-one seemed dull. Her wish to be with Arnie came as an unwanted surprise. It threw her easy adjustment into question. She was used to being herself and didn't want the turmoil of the personal.

She might be able to handle one-on-one with Arnie, as long as she could have group sex on the side. But she knew that as things developed, Arnie wouldn't be able to bear it. She would have to be sneaky or risk losing him. In the past, this wouldn't have been a problem, since new was better than old. But she felt comfortable with Arnie, looked up to him, cared for him, was somehow drawn to him.

She laughed at him too. He wrote articles, reviews, stories. He was preparing to write novels. Why was he so interested in feelings, in what went on between and inside people? She never lost the sense of puppetry in literature. All those people on the page, match-sticks, mannequins. She tucked away her fear of seeing real people like that too, but the truth was she did, at least in part. Orgies, so alive, could be weirdly distant, skeletal people obeying dictates of invisible commands. She dreaded that her depersonalized sense of literature would pervade life.

Arnie meant feelings rather than sensation and brought her up against incapacity. He took her to the place that had clicked off in college. It crossed her mind that she lacked whole areas of personal feeling, but success and sexual excitement more than made up for them. In a way, Arnie was a her she might have been, a missing her, although he had his share of detached indifference as well. Lily did the improbable, if not the impossible: she married him, had children, created a family.

Lily was used to being successful and decided she would be successful at marriage. She could not stop having affairs, but they diminished. She understood sex with Arnie would die and kept it going as long as she could. What she valued with him was priceless, a place, a connection, a life. Children. A price paid by depression controlled by medication.

Even with medication she spent a lot of time in bed, incapacitated. She maintained business ties and made money because she felt driven to. She did what she had to for the children and loved them deeply. This was a great tragedy: she loved but could not *feel* the love! More often than not, she functioned without feeling. She *knew* what had to be done, but joy in doing it was missing. It was enough to get along.

She was in mourning for her life but could not *feel* the loss. Childhood abuse and disruption left permanent scars, injury of her capacity to feel. Good attitudes organized her actions—overall. She did not want to hurt anyone but was deeply hurt with injury she could not come near. Suffering turned off long ago, and a different sort of suffering took its place. Incapacity to suffer feelings can be a tormenting lack. Lily often saw herself as monstrous yet made fun of Arnie for feeling too much, his ludicrous sentimentality. She tried to convince him that practicality was the greatest virtue. But practicality for her went with a void. "Perhaps," she sometimes thought, "I shouldn't have married. But no, I would have fucked my life away. It's a sacrifice I made and don't regret. I wouldn't give up what I have for all the pleasure in the world. I think depression would have caught up with me either way. It was waiting for a chance beneath the excitement and caught me when I slowed down."

Before ending with me once more (she stopped and started a number of times), Lily shared a vision. In the Garden of Eden, there were serpents around the Tree of Life and Tree of Knowledge. A particularly gruesome one—perhaps Lilith—smiled at Eve and Adam and mused, "You're out of here, you know. You'll not stop falling. You'll fall out of pleasure, out of pain, stripped of feeling, a new nakedness. You try to get out of something awful and you keep trying to get out. The new law: Thou shalt try to get out. Where to go? You can't imagine there may never be a there." Lily's face and body meld into the bark of the trees, life and knowledge indistinguishable. Snake fangs and pressure begin to cut and suffocate the trees, bring them down. Only one kind of sensation/feeling is left: chills. One kind of beginning, naked stabs and suffocation.

She felt devoted to her life.

Iris blew the football team in high school, gave blow jobs to bosses at work. She was bright, productive, liked her body, spent a lot of money on its care. She went to business meetings, conferences all over the world, and gave blow jobs to speakers.

She invited me to speak to her colleagues. My turn at last, I thought. I hadn't seen her for years and was fascinated by her tight high smudge of a skirt, smudge of color on her lips, hair teased on end like a cartoon cat electrically shocked.

We touched hands, cheeks. She never married or had children. She was on her own. We went out for coffee and our knees and arms touched. Her clothes were torn, stockings torn. Hands and legs and cheeks bony, stomach fat, There was a smudge of lipstick on her teeth. Tiny breasts limp in a raggy smudge of blouse. I understand this was part of a plan, an image, something that took time to put together, stylish. It was meant to be attractive. She *must* be attractive. She sees lots of men. She is very alive and active.

The more I looked at her the more important family seemed to me. But then I thought of Lily.

I dreamed of Nancy, literally dreamed. In the last dream I had of her, she said yes at last. I waited so long for sex with Nancy. When I imagined it—and there was a time I imagined it often—I felt it through my body, a kind of body soul or fantasy that felt mostly body. It wasn't entirely wholehearted. But intense, real, aching, desirous, lustful.

Endless fantasies, fucking, touching, kissing skin on skin inside-outside, delicious.

It was not to be. A most amazing fact. Many nights I called and we met at bars or restaurants. I would gaze at her fantastic legs, up and down her thighs. One night in particular she wore a tiny leather strap of a thing so high up her thighs my glands never stopped popping. How hungry can you get! It felt so certain. It felt inevitable.

In her apartment, on her couch, getting close but her dog nipped my hand as it moved toward homeland. Where did the dog come from? Out of the bedroom, out of her mind? It wants to be petted. It wants me to leave.

The Nancy in my dream, in my chest, in my cellular body said yes. Could there be any doubt?

The *fact* that it did *not* happen befuddled me for years. A fact like this approaches the unbelievable, makes the unbelievable real. Over the years, I met guys who slept with her. Why them? I hear of a first marriage to a gay guy, a second to a body trainer, a third to a businessman. Decades later she is wealthy, a cancer survivor, her children don't want to see her. She is about to marry a fourth time.

Was I the only guy she said no to?

So close, so far. What would those wonderful moments have been like?

I did have one reservation. Her legs, body, skin totally turned me on. But there was a downturn to her mouth that was blah, not slack exactly, but blah. As if flesh by her mouth escaped being inspirited. In another age, I might call it common, ordinary, unexciting, Brooklyn.

Hey—I live in Brooklyn. Who's calling Brooklyn blah? Well, I didn't live in Brooklyn *then*.

It wasn't just her mouth; it was also her tone, her voice. Something collapsing, not filled out in her tone. Aphanisis found her in her tone of voice. Did she occupy her body more than her voice? Her down-drawn, collapsing mouth? There are many spirits in a person. There are parts I say no to. But is that a reason for her to say no to parts of me that say yes?

I was too intense, nuts, hungry, not sexually appealing to *her*. She sensed *I* was all about me, but that didn't stop her with others. The impassable fact remains: we did not make it, *it* did not happen. A fact that triggered reflection and reverie. It is worth meditating on the sense of disbelief and astonishment concerning things one felt *must* happen but didn't.

I am not saying I got more out of it not happening than I would have if it had happened. I'd vote for the happening and reverie on fulfillment. But the gap between certainty and reality triggered thought for years and has its own kind of mystery.

Absolute certainty—disconfirmed.

The *fact* that Nancy did not sleep with me brings home how powered we are by fantasy. A hallucinatory aspect of lust. I can't tell you how *real* sex with Nancy was in my mind, my imaginings, my desire. Butter in my mouth, my heart, genital-soul happiness.

I rationalized its not happening: I wasn't aggressive enough, good looking enough, not enough in whatever enough would be. Or maybe I was too much in undesirable ways.

How can a feeling be *so* wrong?

Dreamlike certainty is part of reality.

We hallucinate certainty. Certainty is part of hallucination.

In this case, I missed out on a relationship that would not have worked out, with consequences not so great as when leaders of peoples act on and mold others with hallucinated certainties.

We should take the rise of emotional certainty as a signal for humility. We know very little about what goes into experiencing emotional certainty. We do know it is something worth thinking about.

Delusion: thinking is hallucination-free.

What was real with Nancy was hallucinated sex. Not much harm came of it except aggravated loneliness.

When hallucinated war is real, there are dead bodies and broken lives.

If war is avoided, what does one feel one missed? What hallucinatory certainty is frustrated? What gap must be endured?

Nearly seventy, I see hallucinated certainty spreading through experience. Hallucinated identities and reactions to them. Doubt is part of our survival kit, a great tool. Certainty provides raw material to chip away at. Everything contributes.

The hallucinated real adds color to life.

Love for the Inexhaustible past the point of exhaustion helps keep a balance.

That we are hallucinatory beings adds to the struggle to get things right.

Meanings of right: correct, human rights, possession, and the gruesome fact that people are killed and crippled each day, body and soul, because of hallucinated rights. *My* rights over *yours* vs. universal rights.

Garden of Eden. What is it? Genital sensation? Hallucinated perfection, bliss, uninterrupted joy? *Jouissance*? Pure heart? Love?

Lots of not-so-perfect things go on there. A snake plays on envy, stimulates aspiration, aggravates lack. What Eve doesn't have presses over what she has. *Not* grows in the garden. No garden without prohibition. Keep-off-the-tree signs grow in our imaginings. A lust for more and other competing with lust for less, rivalry within the self, inner as well as outer wandering eyes.

We used to see snake as id, God as superego. Boxes crumble, melt. The snake is superego par excellence, persecuting us with who we aren't, with what we don't have. Self-attacker, spoiler, corrupter, player on hubris. Tweaking narcissism, playing deficits. We taunt and haunt ourselves with visions of forever. Comparison machines watching who has what, a subtle smile through it. A competing superego embodied in the Ten Commandments tries to wipe the sneaky smile from our soul. But you can't keep a good snake down. Trickiness is part of survival, part of indirection. Trickiness and law can go haywire, the former turning into a "heh-heh" devil contemptuous and mocking of our efforts: tyrannical, inhumane, losing contact with justice.

The garden is beatific feeling at the heart of life. A feeling crushed and compounded with toxic, damaged stuff. Compacted in misery, horror, tight twists of psychophysical muscle, self-strangulating folds of hate. We separate what life fuses: (1) garden, pain-free state, beatific joy; (2) ordinary living, suffering, labor, struggle; (3) extreme torment, deformation, hell. They are superimposed, coincident, blurred—sometimes teased apart, sometimes more one than the other.

How could we ever have thought the garden trouble-free? Already a hotbed of evil, divisiveness, insoluble difficulty, things get worse. Seeds are sown. The garden is infested with uncontainable strivings, tormenting imaginings. It's just a matter of time. Death, destruction, murder, the whole story—percolating. The ripping apart of the soul is in the garden, in the midst of happiness.

~~~ Tiers or layerings of garden views. One view: lust is basic. Snake as penis, garden as vagina. Melding male-female elements throughout the garden, trees, animals, hints of androgyny, Eve as part of Adam, shadows of prior beings like Lilith lost in myth. Eating the apple, oral sex, sensuality, taste of life. Round fruit can be lots of organs, fleshy curves, as well as circles of time, eternity, and self. Undulating blends.

Sexual aspects of the garden are most popular. For many, it almost seems as if sex is another name for sin, as if something is wrong with pleasure. When Saint Paul says it's better to marry than burn in hell, the latter is understood as burning with sexual desire. Cultural movements put sex on display as if to prove there's nothing wrong with it. Anything is OK that gives you pleasure and doesn't harm another person. And there are cultural tendencies that condemn, even outlaw, certain practices. On both sides of the line, there are gaps between what is said, done, and experienced. It is debatable if anyone escapes conflicted dialectics of pleasure, desire, guilt, shame. It is, after all, in the garden that Adam and Eve suffer opposing tendencies, prohibition, pleasure, aspiration, loss, self-doubt, and worry. Where human beings are, problems arise in the best of conditions.

Another tier involves fear and intensity, not exactly identical with issues of shame and guilt. Lust raises intensity of experience, something we seek and fear. In the middle of a sexual act one may wonder how much pleasure is possible, how much one can take? One opens, draws back, waits, opens some more. One may, at times, hold back out of fear that rising intensity will break one apart. Many speak of fear of surrender. Lust pushes past barriers of self. What starts as a drive to possess can culminate in loss of self. Heightened self-feeling and loss of self go together as well as oppose each other, a paradox we stretch to encompass. Lust brings new life.

A third tier involves riches and poverty of consciousness. Birds of thought flutter around the garden seeding dramas of awareness. Pride and envy spread through carnal, mental, and spiritual dimensions, ushering in what come to seem like competing selves. The challenge to make the best of competing tendencies spreads through history, where too often it seems the worst is unavoidable.

To have knowledge of good and evil, to be like the gods and live forever: isn't it hard enough to become a human being?

Consciousness divided. The idea that a house divided cannot stand gets us off on the wrong track. Division *is* what we work with, and we work with a divided self. I'm even ambivalent about what I think I want. I like you this way, dislike you that way. We can't keep up with consciousness, always behind what mind produces. Add unconscious processes and we're hopelessly bereft, adrift in dumbfounding waters. Freud warned that we're strangers, not masters, in our own house, made up of largely anonymous processes. Travelers in worlds of mind exceeding vision.

Leaving the garden is compared to leaving the womb, a birth out of unconsciousness and indivision. Jung describes an individuation journey toward differentiated wholeness of self. Aspects of psychoanalysis depict psychic hatching processes, growth of awareness of self and other. Some emphasize separation, some connection, some both. I've written of a distinction-union structure that needs double-sided development. We grow in both directions in all sorts of ways. Growth can be helter-skelter rather than in straight lines, with many capacities, in varying degrees, playing a role.

The garden story tidies things up with a rule, a prohibition, which common sense says is made to be broken. To rupture rules opens worlds. Not blindly following authority is part of growing up. So much emphasis in modern life has been on aloneness, as if humankind were emerging from a protective shell. The garden story teaches that trauma is partly a group effort, interplay of subjectivities, crossings of diverse intentionalities, desires, wiles, imaginings, gropings, actions. Evasion of responsibility is contagious. The garden drama is soaked in psychic presence. Nothing can save us from the press of mind, from the challenge of psychic life.

As we grow, let's not leave the garden behind. It's easy to interpret it away Platonically, or as Aristotle did, by emphasizing a hierarchical or developmental scale, ascending from sensory to intellectual life, concrete to abstract. We swing between devaluing and overvaluing one capacity or another. The sensuous garden is part of what gives life good feeling, part of what makes life feel like life. Freud depicted a sensory sea, chaotic and undulating sensory spreads, throughout the body, skin, mucous membranes, unseen organs, nerves, muscles, barely perceptible squeezy movements. Juicy hints rising to scary peaks, threatening ecstasy. Terrifyingly joyful. Flows we cannot convert to meaning support our lives, a background that helps make meaning meaningful.

Nevertheless, the garden is not bereft of cognition. On the contrary, cognition plays a central role, is a prime actor: naming animals, thinking wild thoughts, reaching beyond God's boundaries, beyond God. Mind is in the garden, in the senses.

"The lust of the goat is the bounty of God."

"The nakedness of woman is the work of God."

"Joys impregnate. Sorrows bring forth."

"Sooner murder an infant in its cradle than nurse unacted desires."

"Good is the passive that obeys Reason. Evil is the active springing from Energy."

"Energy is the only life, and is from the Body; and Reason is the bound or outward circumference of Energy."

"Energy is Eternal Delight."

William Blake writes about priests and reason condemning, lacerating, and suppressing body life, impulse, energy. He sided with free love but practiced it only in spirit, in imagination, in declaration. He did not think his marriage could take it. His sex life was lacking, but he cherished his wife. He abided by her wishes, considered her feelings, and remained within the marriage vows.

In vision he sided with lust's bounties. Joy was central. He was joyful on his death bed. He loathed those who tyrannized freedom of spirit. The sense and feel of lust, transmuted through imaginative vision, connected with his intuition of primal energy enlivening body and soul. Lust links with spirit. If spirit is grounded in body, body is an affective, imaginative body, an inspirited body. Yet for Blake it is also or mainly the other way around, body a ray of spirit, part of spirit's glory. Lust is spirit incarnate. Spirit radiates lust's flashes. Enormous intimacy of spirit-body that split off intellect or reason or dogmatic religion or political authority obscures and depletes. A reflective body and energic spirit. We would not have access to the worlds body creates without imaginative vision, imaginative sensation. A new kind of being, hungry for feeling, thought, imagining, part of the life body offers, opening gateways.

"Man has no Body distinct from his Soul; for that call'd Body is a portion of Soul discern'd by the five Senses, the chief inlets of Soul in this age."

Body turns on itself, opens itself to envisionings, an envisioned body.

"For everything that lives is Holy."

Thus sings the chorus in the last words of *The Marriage of Heaven and Hell*, Blake's paean to the wedding of opposites in imaginative vision. A song to life.

The devil is holier than the priest, insofar as the former transmits life energy and the latter kills it. Everything in the garden is holy: the snake, fruit, man and woman, tight-assed/tight-fisted God prohibiting part of his bounty, jealous of the life he bestows.

All part of life, like Greek gods, rich with conflict.

Blake's priests today: All those who know, all who are right. A smug face at the head of a nation. What would a face rich in life look like?

⁓ To turn a heart of stone into a heart of flesh: where does lust come in?

⁓ Psychoanalysis presents difficulties on the path to lust. You'd think it would be simpler—libido, eros, sex drive. Psychoanalysis parses it into components. Drives made up of partial drives. Oral, anal, phallic, genital, active, passive, exhibitionistic, voyeuristic, sadistic, masochistic—facets of sexuality. Seeing, hearing, smelling, over and underneath skin, movements gross and subtle. Physical thrills, psychic shivers. Located where? You can almost locate sensations as they ripple and spread, but the feel of the whole remains ineffable. Sometimes it is in the organ, and you know very well which organ or sets of organs. But it spreads, diffuses, reaches new places you didn't know about, organless places, dimensions beyond organs that organs ignite, that feeling ignites. Do you hunger more for sensation you can pin down or for ineffable sensation?

⁓ Sensation *is* ineffable.

⁓ Where does sex start? Or is it more like a cable computer connection, always on, ready for use, and body parts tune into it?

⁓ Lacan is dramatic. He states that the whole sexual drive is located nowhere. There is no whole sexual drive. There are partial drives, partial sexual experiences. The sex drive—the whole sexual thing—is unreal. It is made up of currents, crosscurrents, eddies, swirls, impulse, counter-impulse. Conflict, dialectic, diversity in the drives. Drives are subsets of drives. Desire = groups of desires.

What are psychoanalysts thinking when they say, "Follow your desire." Which desire, which subfactor? Which part of which part? What a chimera, threading the needle from desire to desire.

A Buddhist says, "Cut desire at the root!" The desire to undercut desire.

Cut desire at the root and the snake multiplies. Everywhere it is cut it multiplies. Roots are tangles. There is no single root.

Psychoanalytic schools proliferate like angels on the head of a pin. What are they looking for? What is psychoanalytic desire, psychoanalytic lust? Snakes of desire, psychoanalytic snakes.

We have established that the garden is a packed garden, far from trouble-free. It is alive with desire for Other and More. Lack, insufficiency are built in. The promise to children, the lie, the wish, the fantasy: I'll give you everything you want, if . . . All you have to do is . . .

Love songs: you're my everything, my all.

Mystical promise: union with God is all.

Today totalities make us claustrophobic. We want more from God, from a lover. We want something more or other, something different from all.

We want something partial.

We are getting tired of the race for the delusional all. Even though we are still totality addicts, we seek fine grain, details. We are getting frightened of a propensity to cover things with hallucination, delusion. Perception dips into fantasy, fantasy into hallucination, hallucination into delusions of wholeness, completion, totality, certainty. How do we cut ourselves loose from hallucinatory wholes? Cut heads off, hearts out? What do we aim at by cutting? Cut delusion out of us? And the delusion of being delusion-free? A schizophrenic dreams of cut flowers, bleeding flowers. A poem cuts reality, quickens reality. Living in the cut of a poem, I think, for a moment, delusion stops. I stop breathing, breathe faster. Someone whispers, "Parts can't stay parts."

Fantasy supports desire. Hallucination supports fantasy. Desires dip into hallucination.

Lacan gives as an example Freud's daughter's dream of food. Literal enough for a child. When I ask a pet lover, what is her dog dreaming, "Food," she might say. Understandable enough for common sense.

But Freud and Lacan involve uncommon sense. Freud connects libido, impulse, desire, primary process with hallucination. For example, his fiction: when an infant is hungry, she hallucinates a breast, a fulfilling feed, perhaps a beatific feed. "Impulse is satisfied essentially by hallucination."

Desexualized reality cannot satisfy the drive. Mere reality is lacking. Hallucinatory surplus is filling. Impulse does not *just* seek satisfaction, it seeks satisfaction tinged with hallucinatory fulfillment. With something more than mere satisfaction. Satisfaction is not completely satisfying. It is hallucinatory totality that adds the extra something. That adds something even to a child's dream of food!

When Freud said that little children are sexual, he was affirming something about psychic life that was sexual. A sexual psyche. When little Anna dreams of food, a tart, eggs, strawberries, these are not just objects of need. They are treats, teats, delectable, libidinal. They are the more of the body and the fantasy body, the libidinal drive and play of the mind. They have psychic taste, the taste of the psyche. Food is not just food, it is laced with desire, pleasure, satisfaction and the more that hallucination provides.

For food to appear in a Freudian dream (relatively early Freud), it must be sexualized, forbidden—the apple in the garden—and, therefore, food for hallucination. This tells us that an awful lot of hallucination goes on in the garden and we can see the serpent as a master of delusion, of hallucinatory desire. Is all desire hallucination or hallucination-prone? All Freudian desire, perhaps, especially in the hands (the lips, the tongue, the mouth, the voice) of the master serpent, Lacan.

"It is only on account of the sexualization of these objects that the hallucination of the dream is possible—for, as you will notice, little Anna only hallucinates forbidden objects." "It is from the point at which the subject desires that the connotation of reality is given in the hallucination."

Where drive is, hallucination is. A sexual psyche, a hallucinatory psyche. Lust, then, is on the side of hallucination and turns reality into dream. It is not just sex we want, but hallucinated sex. Without delusions about what sex is, sex would have a hard time filling our sails. To live up to its billing, sex has to be more than sex. Freudian-Lacanian sex *is* more: sex is always, in some sense, hallucinated sex.

One of the great themes of psychoanalysis is how we try to substitute total for partial satisfaction. Satisfaction is always partial. Hallucination-delusion makes it total. Total for a time, if at all, since desire drives hallucination, and while hallucination puts a nipple in desire's mouth, the force of the drive continues unabated, only apparently fobbed off. The force of drive is constant, part of psychic circuits outside of need. In the realm of the forbidden, no garden can be enough.

Hunger as physiological need may be satisfied by food. But impulse, drive, desire requires hallucinatory satisfaction—that is, reaches beyond any possible satisfaction. Reaches beyond the real.

It is hard to pinpoint the physiology of lust, but there is such a thing as physical satisfaction—which may or may not do much for the constant force of desire and its hallucinated feeds. Physiology and fantasy slip in and out of each other. Sometimes they cohere or give the illusion of cohering, which makes us think they *ought* to cohere more. Fitting together slides into hallucination of totality, which throws us off the scent of what people have to do to get along together.

〰️ "In the subject who, alternately, reveals himself and conceals himself by means of the pulsation of the unconscious, we apprehend only partial drives. The *ganze Sexualstrebung,* the representation of the totality of the sexual drive, is not to be found there, Freud tells us."

Again, only partial drives. The whole sexual thing, the representation of the totality of the sexual drive—when you look at it closely, there are parts, this and that crosscurrent, this and that meaning, clumps of meaning. This is one reason Lacan calls the unconscious elusive, ambiguous, equivocal. One reason sexuality slips through our psychic fingers. One confuses *it* with objects, objects with finality.

A reason for the famous transience of lust is that sexual meanings are in flux, objects change meanings (become different sorts of signifiers), arousal (urges, drivenness, impetus) changes meaning. In a single sex act, object or libido may assume different shapes, more exciting, less exciting, driven by contingent shifts of meaning as the act progresses or ebbs and flows. The term, "single sex act," is misleading, since a multitude of nuances are disclosed when one becomes sensitive to temporal pulsation.

Is it still with amazement that we come upon the realization that arousal is driven by unconscious meaning? By what the other means to me or I mean to the other? Driven by scenarios inscribed throughout my body, a lettered body, a body driven by meaning?

〰️ Isn't there a sense of the whole, a feeling for the whole? As when one says, "That was beautiful." "That was bad." "That was great." "That was exciting." "That was nothing, deadening." "I'm sorry I did it." "I'm glad I did it." People say things like that all the time—good sex, bad sex. Surely, there is a sense of the whole, a thread that runs through it. A main affective thread that sums up the atmosphere other affective threads bounce around in.

When we look at wholes and see parts, is this a bit like thinking we can't get from here to there if each time we move we go half the distance? We dissolve any object into texture and chaos by staring at it without blinking long enough. We can make any object lose form by losing ourselves in bits of it.

We are at the mercy of shifts of focus. Parts made of wholes, wholes of parts. Ancient notion: micro ↔ macro. Modern artists open the body. Smooth beauty of skin and facial features simultaneously opening to inside organs, flesh, bones. Seeing outside-inside together, as if they are interchangeable or support and suppress each other, surprise each other. The older reversible figure-ground, beauty-hag. Life and death inside-outside each other, as if reversible.

Wholes grab us. Parts grab us. The spirit of the whole, spirits of parts.

Are we paranoid about death? Inside lust we see death. At the same time, lust tries to transcend death. Sometimes succeeds. Pleasure at its maximum outflanks death—as in a fantastic moment, the greatest moment, where orgasmic fulfillment propels one past orgasm into the heavens, past the stars, past what organism can support. Skin opening, heart opening, brain flashing. All together, the best moment ever. I never thought that . . . it could be this way. Again, again. A peak of consciousness worth it all. A moment that beats death, leaves death behind.

Such moments are real, among the most real of all. Still, there is room for deconstruction. I never thought that it could be like that. Well, that is just what I hoped for, just what I dreamt, wished, awaited. I didn't expect it, I say. But it is precisely what I did expect.

I have been thinking such a moment for years. I have felt this moment in my skin, underneath images, formlessly spreading, enfolding, catapulting. I have been living in it without experiencing it as such. It informs my life, an ideal moment beyond moments. What I live for.

Freudian-Lacanian paranoia is important, protective. If not exactly realistic, it maintains an important cautionary take on things, bordering on prudence. The old saw: nothing is as it seems. X might also be Y might also be Z. Might also be. No last word, no final resting point. No absolute, no totality. Keep your eye on what else is happening, the universe's sleights of hand, sleights of mind.

To subject the genital drive "to the circulation of the Oedipus complex"—one of the greatest disappearing tricks of all. Genital drive—we know what that means, anyone who feels tumescence does. We *think* we know what that means. Until culture gets its hands on it. Subject the drive to kinship structures. *Not* mother, *not* father. *Not*—oh, back in the garden again. Oh, that drive, where is it going?

Lacan tells us, as the drive filters through culture it dissolves and reappears as defined by culture. We learn from others what it is, what is isn't. Do we know what sex is by ourselves? Others tell us what it is in important ways that stamp us. To what extent is sexuality conditioned? Conditioned by meanings others give it, by another's desire? The whole sexual thing—*ganze Sexualstrebung*—gets built up out of others' desires, identifications with how others see our sexual being. The whole sexual thing, the drive, has complex infrastructures. Lacan calls the drive a montage of partial drives, other desires, identifications.

The idea of a whole drive is, partly, a fiction dissolved by culture, fabricated by culture. "The *ganze Sexualstrebung* is nowhere apprehensible in the subject. Yet because it is nowhere, it is nevertheless diffused, and it is this Freud is trying to convey to us." Sex as everywhere, anywhere, not confined to this or that organ. A very sexy universe, a sexy psyche, exceeding the bounds of organs, since the latter take on different meanings, different tonalities, colors, nuances, changes of function, infused by their meaning for the Other. We seek ourselves as we dissolve in the signifying roles of sex and culture.

Lacan spotlights the subject as constituted through meanings given by the Other. This includes sexuality, the sexual subject, lust as constituted by meanings others give it. "The subject as such is uncertain because he is divided by the effects of language. Through the effects of speech, the subject always realizes himself more in the Other, but he is already pursuing more than half of himself. He will simply find his desire ever more divided, pulverized, in the circumscribable metonymy of speech."

Sexuality is always displaced, moving from and going to somewhere else. Always meaning something else, partly circumscribed by past meaning, laced with future meanings not yet discovered. The subject is subject to the Other, the Other's desire, comprehension, culture, language. Lacan tracks paranoia of influence, one's very own sexuality unconsciously driven by its meaning for others. In this we are claustrophobic partners, trying to get out of our definitions of each another.

We imagine lust will break through. We'll ride waves of desire out of the prison of meaning. Elation of getting out, breaking free. Lust's joy.

Part of lust's depression is falling back into the meanings that compose it. The dim realization that it is made up of what one tries to escape, that a certain alienation is part of its make-up. One tries to break free from what one can't break free from. Part of why the momentary freedom of violence is illusory, imaginary. There is no getting rid of the speaking subject, no sex without meaning. Neither sex nor violence can make meaning go away, although it can try.

〜 Sea of *jouissance*. Sea of meaning.

Lust and violence create meaning as well as disperse it.

When meaning suffocates, dispersal begins?

A pendulum?

Meaning and dispersal never stop—meaning in dispersal, dispersal in meaning, inside each other.

What can freedom mean? Finding an outside?

〜 Persecuted by meaning. Lust and violence displace one form of persecution with another. For a moment, persecution is dissolved. An illusion? A negative hallucination, hallucinating persecution as not there? Freud says creative work stands a better chance.

〜 The cut of language, signifying beings, bodies as signifiers. Sex signifies. Lust has meaning, is made up of meanings. It does not take place in a cultural vacuum, in a life without language, a meaningless life. No self without a language context. Lacan believes this displaces us into the field of the Other. The subject arises in the field of the Other, traversing language, parental culture, the unconscious. No psychic birth without influence.

To be a signifier for others, as others are signifiers for us, places (displaces) us into fields of interpenetrating meanings, with no beginning, no end. What we mean to others, what others mean to us. What we mean to ourselves because of what we mean to others. One of Lacan's formulas: we desire the desire of the Other. We mold to capture the other's desire. The influence of desire, melding to what we mean to each other or fail to mean. Desire is not culturally vacant but travels along gradients of meaning.

To live through the cut of language is to live as lack. The abundance of meaning premises lack. Not just the gap between consciousness and nature, loss of solidity, loss of thingness (these certainly play a role in and out of the garden). Lack that meaning circumscribes in itself, creates by its own existence. We can always mean something else. Meaning, like time, is on the move, happening over and under us, inside and outside of itself.

We try to absolutize ourselves through meaning, make meaning mean one thing. A kind of fundamentalist literalism, fundamentalism of identity. We may succeed in slowing meaning down, slowing ourselves down. But the possibility of revelation, overturning, accretion, renewal remains. We can always mean something else to ourselves and others.

This is a plenitude, a bounty premised on a lack.

Lack as part of the structure of bounty.

The movie *In America* has one sex scene, a beautiful sex scene. The husband/father, blindfolded, chases his children, two daughters. A game they love. He thinks of his dead son and forces himself to go on, although there is a hole in his being, a hole in life. His daughters squeal with pleasure, although they share this hole too, in their particular ways.

His wife notes that he does not chase *her*, does not find her. She is left out of the chase, not part of his desire. He realizes his ellipsis, tries to make up for it, goes after her, says he can *always* find her, find her *anywhere*. The play of desire and its lack, making up for its lack, a rise or promise of plenitude against a hole in being. The atmosphere heightens. Sexual arousal hinges on layers of unconscious meaning. Blind chase, energy, a vulnerable desperation running through childhood quickens desire.

She sends her daughters to get ice cream at the nearby store called Heaven. They know what she means. Her husband is the last to know.

While he blindly chases, she disrobes. When, finally, they embrace, the heavens storm. Lightning, pouring rain, thunderous sound. The scene switches to an artist who lives downstairs. We are led to think he is mad and caught in an emotional storm. He slashes himself, sprinkles blood, presses a bloody hand print on his canvas. Meanwhile, the girls eat ice cream, loving the storm as they watch it through the store window. The sex act mounts, mounts. An outpouring of their lives, of loss.

The loss of their son, the main thing. But also lack of money, lack of a decent life, immigrants trying to make a go of it in a new country, aliens amid degradation, hardship, adrift. For the moment, lacks and loss and anguish pour into the beauty of sex. In another moment, new levels of lack appear, new challenges, despair, worry, inspiration.

A kind of alchemy, crushed feeling, crushed meaning, rage, love, birth of fierce vulnerability, transmission of spirit, not just of blood.

Death as Other. Lack superimposed on lack. Lacan is insistent: with sex comes death. Sex, a fall into death. "The living being, by being subject to sex, has fallen under the blow of individual death." As if one lowers oneself, subjects (subjugates) oneself to the reproductive cycle and discovers "the essential affinity of every drive with the zone of death." Doubleness. Sexuality as signifier of life and death. Lack does not simply pulse through meaning; it characterizes life, which we live in a signifying way. For us life is not only life; it takes on meaning, many meanings. At times, it vaporizes into meanings.

A line of religious thought involves the idea that one can outmaneuver death by abstaining from sex. By negating the reproductive chain, we unite our soul with life eternal. Saint Augustine's wrenching account of his struggle with lust. Concupiscence vs. faith: to raise spirit and win eternal life. The association of flesh, carnality, reproduction with death, sin (you die from sin), lower, weak.

In America takes another direction. Sex is wonderful but does not evade doubleness. It is part of the mix that plunges you deeper into the swirl, the life of life, grief, joy, beauty haunted by death, loss part of fullness, fullness part of loss. The plunge into life, the affirmation, is what gives the movie its impetus, against the ground of disease, grief, deformation. Life shines through death.

The husband is shocked into emotional death by the death of his son, the link between sex and death made palpable. He now must journey into life, and sex is one of the portals. Neither sex nor death will be the same, as he gradually gathers a sense of what living means.

In psychoanalysis, it sometimes seems that life becomes a death symbol. Echoes of religious terror. Life as death symbol—often true, if not ubiquitous.

It is not clear that seeing how pervasively death operates in the life of meaning will make things better. But it is clear that not seeing death's fusion with pleasure (e.g., blood lust) will make things worse. The pull of destructive pleasures is enormous, lust a main channel. Lust spreads like butter through human strivings, melting deep into aggressive fantasy and action.

Lust as part of murder as well as murder as part of lust. Note the love-death theme in literature and war. Inspiring, filling, thrilling to some, blood-curdling, chilling to many. Laughter of death disguised as love. Death takes a mask off, shows its grimace in war, substituting the mask of heroism for the lover. Lust-death of heroism. Hero worship—suicide.

Lack in Lacan, life's fall from life, life becoming real. His vision of originary lack, which he calls unreal: pure life, lacking real life. One must appreciate the quirky maliciousness of his turn of thought, to posit unreal fullness as the lack of lacks. Libido, pure life instinct, life going on, life without death, without falling into sexed reproduction. What can be more unreal, more lacking? Unreal life, lacking real life.

In a way, the husband/father in *In America* was living this pure life, life without death (not without sex, although sex as life was not yet part of death) before the death of his son. His son's death shocked him out of life. Out of life without death. The pure life Lacan posits. Unreal life.

The movie sets the challenge of linking life with death, the impossible with the real. Can one grow into living? Can one survive life—the shock of death? How? With what quality? In what way? As a dead person? A mad person? A growing, real person? What does living mean?

꙳ Lacan sees symbols of completion as an attempt to reclaim deathless life. Life before generative sex. The breast, the placenta, the mother, the teddy bear, the lover, the work of art—partial attempts to glue self to life unending. Perhaps if we represent death intensely enough, it will go away. We will be deathless again. We will be pure life again.

What is the part of himself the individual loses at birth? What is the loss of loss that separation symbolizes? One of Lacan's answers: deathless life. The unreal par excellence. "The breast—as equivocal, as an element characteristic of the mammiferous organization, the placenta, for example—certainly represents that part of himself that the individual loses at birth, and which may serve to symbolize the most profound lost object. I could make the same kind of reference to all other objects." The most profound lost object, not simply the breast, placenta, mother, self: life without end in total fullness. The unreal.

That which lust seeks to fill in, to transcend, to create, to bring to pass. As if the intensity of lust, if full and long and complete enough, will make life live. Will make life live forever. To fuck death out of life. To fuck the unreal out of life.

꙳ "We had great sex. Great sex!" Gary said repeatedly. He told me this for weeks. Months. A new woman friend. He could hardly believe his luck. She wants to do everything. She wants *everything*. As close to maximum desire as he ever knew. She is appreciative of his every move, he of hers. She is totally beautiful.

There were reservations from the beginning, but he brushed them aside. An inner voice wanted to go slow, but he didn't listen. Marge wanted it all and fast, total fullness. And she knew how to create it. He felt himself drawn in, a kind of passive current, an undertow, and he gave in. Willingly. He jumped in. Ignoring part of himself, a part he didn't want to know.

Marge and Gary maximized desire, maximized pleasure. Did she have a counter-voice too, one not listened to? We don't link up with all our whispers. We can't connect with a lot of what goes on, too much too fast. Later, when something we didn't want to see or hear forces its way into preeminence, we realize its time has come.

Gary fought the counter-pull for several years, although its first, grievous, dramatic appearance was roughly half a year into the relationship. Marge gave him a blow job in a boat, music in the background, moonlight, starlight, soft breezes. Perfection. And he didn't enjoy it, didn't feel a thing. He was appalled by his indifference. He wouldn't care if she stopped. She intensified her efforts to make it better. In principle, he knew *it* was good. *She* was good. He would never have it better. This was as good as it gets. And he felt nothing. Died out.

He was dumbfounded and kept protesting, "But it was great. It was great—and I didn't feel a thing. I couldn't get into it." His cock remained hard and he came, but the air came out of his spirit. He didn't understand himself.

For a time, a long time, he tried to push past his resistance, not give into the downside. What was taking the life out of life? Everything sexually he ever wanted—thought he wanted—his catalogue of desires fulfilled—and he was increasingly empty.

He had many rationalizations. He was good at the interpretative game. "I can't take too much goodness. I need to punish myself, hold back, pull back." A penitential ideology. Too attached to mother's admiration. Too attached to mother's criticism. Too angry at mother's narcissism. Fear of toxic attachment, loss of self. Fear of life.

He mistrusted his negativity and tried to push himself into life. Forced himself to stay with Marge, to have sex. How could he give it up? But the inner turn occurred, and it was just a matter of linking up with it. A few more years.

Marge became angry at more and more things, the way he dressed, ate, behaved, breathed. She blamed him for *her* not wanting to go to bed with *him*. She turned off when his spirit died. The death of his desire walloped her insides. There is direct transmission of feelings, although we mask it with words, faces, gestures.

Gary tried to justify himself. There was something in her he couldn't put his finger on, something in her spirit, something to blame. She was too controlling, too sure, masterful. Too desperate. After all, her husband left after ten years of marriage, walked without warning. He said something about not recognizing himself in his life with her. She created a life, a home that wasn't his. Strange note of passivity from a successful man. Marge kept telling Gary, "We had sex every day, every single day for ten years."

Things happen, and we don't understand them. We get lots of ideas, especially in therapy, but do we really know?

Marge knew from the outset she was not going to live with Gary. She was not going to leave the place she perfected over the years and she did not want him in it for long periods of time. She added him to her life like seasoning, hoping he'd blend in. He thought it was his lack of commitment that kept them apart and was astonished to discover that she had her own agenda. She had her life and interests and wanted him in it as enrichment, not a center. He suspected it was his peripheral status that dampened his spirit. He thought he wanted more, but could *he* give more? My suspicion was that Gary and Marge were stymied by unrecognized personality limitations, readily blaming the other out of their own unknown deficits. The beauty of sexual urgency was supposed to fill in blanks of self-knowledge? Too big a burden for lust to keep up with.

Lacan speaks of a fading, disappearance, dying associated with meaning: "When the subject appears somewhere as meaning, he is manifested elsewhere as 'fading,' as disappearance." As one becomes what one means to another, one disappears or dies to or as oneself. We, constituted in a field of influence, are given to ourselves as someone else. Rimbaud's famous, "I am another."

A fallacy or limitation of paranoid truth, dread of influence: we are enriched, supported, extended by relationships. We grow through mutual impact and response. Now let's add the lethal ingredient. Part of growth is premised on multifaceted loss. As religion teaches, we lose to find. What do we gain and lose as signifiers, beings who mean something, stamped by what we mean?

We often relate our loss to loss of vital contact. By becoming speaking beings, we access life through what it means to us. Life filtered through meaning. Life as signifying life, all that life might mean—a kind of fading, disappearing of life as such by becoming symbolizing beings. Life mediated by signifying processes. Signifying processes structured by language, parent, society, the unconscious, the Other.

We are caught between double madness and double disappearance, between hypersymbolization and flight from symbols, the drive to return to the thing itself, life as such. Lust breaks through hypersymbolization, then falls into undertows of meanings it tries to clear. We disappear behind and through ourselves, not able to make lust or meaning hold still.

Death is not only part of life; it obsesses life. How much life does it possess? How much life escapes it? Lacan uses the term "aphanisis," harking back to Ernest Jones's depiction of the disappearance of desire, now applying it more generally and fatefully to the disappearing subject. The subject who disappears as she is constituted through language. A disappearing that is part meaning. A dying that is part of being born as a signifier. We may seek to disclose ourselves through meaning but discover our necessary disappearance as well.

Physical death becomes a symbol of more elusive deaths, some more horrifying than merely dying. Deaths of self, personality, strivings, one's sense of being. Humans, throughout history, achingly, hysterically, desperately try to magnify through symbolic awareness deaths they go through and fear, portrayal after portrayal of what one death process or another does to living souls. As if saying, "Look what happens, look what happens," trying to call attention to what we go through, what life does to us. As if calling to each other, exchanging messages, trauma notes will make a difference in our helplessness. Our silent cry as we solidify/vaporize into signifiers.

The subject tries to free himself of the signifier's aphanisic effect, make disappearance go away, will death to die. To will aphanisis away, to delete lack, is one of the strangest lacks of all. The correlative notion is that life is, or should pulse with, absolute fullness, life replete with life. Therefore, no pulse at all, since pulse is variation, more life, less life, more death, less death. Or perhaps variation within life, variation within death.

One way of getting rid of death, too prevalent, is to turn people into signifiers of death and try to kill off those signifiers. Wipe out death by wiping out death's signifiers. For example, Jews as lethal infection threatening the death of Germany. Get rid of death by killing Jews. Make life better by getting rid of death carriers, the meaning of death, death's infection. Turn life into super-life, all-life. There is truth to B movies depicting twisted, lustful Nazi faces trying to rid themselves of soul infection by murder, a war of signifiers in which bodies die. An inverse process, in which signifiers are turned into bodies, bodies into signifiers, and people die.

The rush is to extremes: get rid of all signs of death, all local signifiers that take life away from life. There is a great hallucinatory drive to get death out of the system, to make life only life. Life's sense of life without death, Lacan's life as signifier of deathless life, the unreal. A lack of lacks, since deathless life lacks the real. The ultra-fundamentalist Christian right, wanting Jews to control the West Bank to hasten the Rapture. Nothing causes more death than lust for unalloyed life. Life wishes death away, surely. But more lethally, it is a death drive that wishes death away.

Lust has its own aphanisis, is not exempt from the structure it tries to evade. Behind lust is the disappearing subject. One pours all one can into focused life for moments. Revving life to what the open throttle can take. Hoping behind hope to disappear disappearance. Discovering all life long that invisibility is not negotiable.

To make peace with not being there. Is that possible?

Abundance, overflow masks aphanisis.

It is not that there is only death. To be drunk with life is real. But in this drunkenness, this great gift—aphanisis. How could Gary and Marge not know what hit them? The fading involved in lust was with them all their lives, disappearance a part of every life sensation. A disappearing subject in every life-feeling ever felt.

It took Gary by surprise in the middle of a blow job. Not only acute awareness of lack of desire, sexual feeling, sensation, but a more total aphanisis of spirit, of personification. Against his conscious will and wishes, he found himself not in it, not a part of what was happening. Rather, too apart, there as someone not there, a ghostly and ghastly observer, disheartened, disappointed, chagrined. Perhaps he needed disappointment in the midst of plenty, needed plenty to diminish.

It may also be that aphanisis needed to take a more compelling form in the face of efforts to shut it out. Marge and Gary's wish to create a perfect experience made a missing something (no-thing) more acute. For Gary, it happened all at once in the middle of a dream come true, the perfect blow job. To feel nothing when something he fantasized actually happened. He was not prepared for such radical failure and the invitation to self-confrontation. No wonder he tried to whisk it away as an effect of guilt, prohibition, resistance to life, inner persecution, a protective need to spoil, mixed with incipient, complementary realism—maybe life is not what it's cracked up to be.

Mini-suicide in the middle of sex. There *are* people who *do* kill themselves in the downturn, the downspin of spirit, when they fail (inevitably) to maintain life at valued peaks, or when they are hit by the awful discovery that valued peaks do not end insufficiency or even make up for it. No suicide for Gary or Marge—life means too much, both are *in* life—but bafflement at a loss of aliveness, air going out of their psychological balloon. Almost instantaneously, Gary's penis changes values, from life to death. No problem with impotence. The problem was potency without life, function without spirit. Lights went out inside, and he could not connect with himself, with Marge, with the link his body might have made.

Surely Gary's (and Marge's) trauma history played a roll in this pass. But emphasis here is on a general structure that crosses many kinds of histories. The attempt to jam life into life, make life only life, is too much to sustain. The sex act was to signify completion, totality, happiness, wish-fulfillment, the perfect real, life without death. Gary maintained organ erection but lost erection of spirit. The inner phallus dropped through a psychic hole, a hole in the signifier, a lacuna no reality can undo. Evading the ever-missing has repercussions. No amount of pumping oneself up can fill the hole in meaning.

People do many things to pump up life past death. Those who die while mountain climbing, for example. They almost ride exhilaration, challenge, thrill, and skill over death, but sometimes they slip. Like something suddenly slipping away in Gary. Getting to the top, the climax—to make time stand still, to make life only life, super-life. "To get the most out of life" is a common phrase, a widespread bit of bitterness, tragedy waiting to happen.

Recent stock scandals, the overreaching of big business, fraud, self-entitlement at the expense of others: not totally unlike Gary's click-off in the middle of a triumphant dream. Deceit in the highest branches of government in order to get one's way, burgeoning psychopathy where winning is all, paid for by soaring debt and dread of collapse, deflation, injury. Paid for by murder. Death for the sake of profit.

Not just war as an instrument of policy. A few deaths in tests, some debilitating repercussions as a by-product of medications that affect mood, a small price for helping many and a productive economy. Wealth is a heady business and something clicks off to maintain this high. Aphanisis, ever present, eclipsed for a time by wealth's lust for more. To fill life with life without missing death's absence. Megalomanic loss of the sorrow that is part of humane spirit.

The eternal Jonah, seeing no satisfactory outcome, flees, unable to find a godless spot, a deathless spot.

Would things have gone better had Gary and Marge allowed for something missing all along? Do we need to get used to something missing a bit at a time, as part of each moment? The death in meaning, something not there—can the urgent need for sexual beauty allow for something missing? If only.

Ifs are cruel, pollyannaish, accusatory.

What a gift Freud gave us—a new codification of impulse, a new permission, a wider awareness. We are all kinds of streamings, impulses, polyvalent, split, diffuse, concentrated, intense, fluctuating. Homo/heteroerotic, oral, anal, urethral, genital, over/underside of skin, touch inside and outside, upper, lower, through one's being. All senses are a kind of touching. Touch everywhere.

Mind orgasms, body orgasms, spiritual orgasms.

In letters to Fliess, Freud links creativity with sublimated homoerotic libido. Everything contributes.

Marie Coleman Nelson once remarked that any human being

alone in a room with anything thinks of sex. Everything is filled with sexual possibilities.

Vegetables, animals, inanimate objects. The phrase: "He has sex on his brain."

Child sexual abuse is a horrific crime. The wonder is that there is not more of it, although there is more than we believe. Many people remember sex beginning in childhood, some kind of sexual atmosphere.

It's a wonder we can think at all. Then again, perhaps sex helps us think. To know someone, all the ways to know.

Psychoanalysis links curiosity with sexuality (where do babies come from? what do mommy and daddy do? what feels so good or disturbing or . . . ?). Not that curiosity is reduced to sexuality. Reductionism is useful but delusional. Can one separate capacities, as if sex is one thing, thinking another? I am a sexual thinking being, a thinking, feeling sexual being. When I lose my head which head is lost? Does thinking vanish or do I find it surfacing inside my orgasm? Orgasms bless thinking, even if the latter runs away with itself. It is exciting, if hard, to think. Thinking: one of the great, secret turn-ons. Is anything more exciting than meaning? The thrill of meaning?

Sex gets part of its thrill by what it means, its function as signifier. Signifying caring, recognition, desire, value, affirmation, wholeness, completion, victory.

Sex makes believe there is nothing but life.

It almost achieves such a moment and aims at it again and again. All my youth I tried finding this moment over and over, wondering how there could be anything else.

One and one makes two only in abstract thinking. In real life it means three or four or more, coupling, generating, birth, family, children, rivals. Numbers arise in a psycho-social-sexual matrix. Counting warriors. What comes out of bodies, what does away with bodies. The sexual roots of mathematics, fecundity, the addition, multiplication, and division of birth, the subtraction of death. The one, the many, nothing. Part of a fever we try to transcend or try to give in to.

What an amazing thing, to think we are separate from our minds.

Freud wrote of the ego as a sort of psychic monogamy or monotheism, unifying sensory streaming, gathering autoerotic fields together through I-sensation.

Great god I, impervious, sensitive, magnificent, cringing in the face of turbulence that wipes me out from within.

The great discovery of recovery, greater by being wiped out: rising, regrouping, reforming. I'ing, dying, re-I'ing. Do you remember when you first met a terror of undoing, then became undone and came back again, and again? Do you remember when you did not quite come back?

Few things are more impressive than such experiences.

You watch and breathe into the break and return. You are a sea of waves and mirrors breaking. Self, a new toy, the feel of sapiens sentient. You go on forever and then you end forever. When you end you *think* it is forever. You scream and go under and come back in amazement thinking sunrise. It doesn't stop but something stops you. You hate yourself for not spending more time going into it.

You hate yourself for not spending more time in it but fear the screaming, a mind-bending music on the other side of the void. Another side of a world. Of worlds. Far sides. Then you snap. That's what they call madness. Snapping out of place. But they also speak of snapping as elastic, snapping into place. You snap out of and into place, again and again. Out of and into keep changing. Place changes. You snap here again, as if nothing happened, but you feel differences.

That elastic pop and stretch is what lust is after, popping and stretching the body thin and tight all over the world, so that world-skin dissolves through its pores, and pores are all that's left, pores that are sensations. There's no room for anything else.

It is like Noah's great flood without an ark, and one is surprised at peeps of consciousness like birds and rabbits and worms after the great flood. A mountain climber opens his eyes after falling into an abyss or someone attempting suicide comes to in a hospital, ambushed by a ticking I after imagining it was gone.

The ticking is like a gnat or fly buzzing under your nose. You keep clutching, swinging at it even while you remember that it is part of you, that it *is* you. Your horse tail can't get rid of it. It survives every storm.

Can you peel the skin of an orange without getting juice on your fingers? Some people can. Some people can eat an orange without having it squirt. It seems a desirable thing to be able to do if you don't want to get sticky. Most of us never master the art of staying dry, no matter how hard we try.

I heard someone speak of the universe as a giant orange that we live inside although we imagine that we are on the outside skin. Even when we think we are dry we are wet. There is no unsticky state. Of course, the orange is circular, so we have to think of it being sort of cushy and squeezy, so that shape is funny and capable of shifts. Kind of a juicy universe, skin mixed with juice and pulp, squooshy and moving. A pulpable universe. You think its solid when the squoosh moves very slowly, slow being funny.

Some like it slow, some like it fast, some don't know what they like.

Lacan is so adamant about desire as a nodal point of the psyche because most of us don't know what we want much of the time. Desire defends against uncertainty and the fear that identity keeps shifting. It is not our desire for mastery that is the great secret but our desire for anonymity. The fact that we want to pass through the world anonymous is scary. Lust for identity saves us from a desire to be free. Psyche keeps forming around us, around our anonymous core. Saved from a desire for nothingness by a desire for complicity. The force that is part of lust, like will to power or dominance, is motored by delicious complicity: power squeezes, sucks the juice of complicity. The force of lust lifts us for a time. Freedom of pleasure, obliteration, saturation, the gas of sensation. For a moment, aliveness wins. At least this I can be sure of: I lust, therefore I am; I am, therefore I lust. But I tend to vanish if lust opens up and heavens open within it, not exactly the biblical heaven within, but a close cousin.

The one and the many, plurality in the one: a theme of depth psychology as well as philosophy and religion. One name of God means plurality, another means one. I'ing and the amazing universe of self and body swimming through the I: the one and only I, the singular-plural I. Freud has obsessively impassioned portrayals of this plural one, fanning out of impulses through hide-and-seeking I. I with over-under, pleasure-real divisions and always more. Today writers enjoy portraying I with horizontal and vertical splits. We might have it easier if proliferation of splitting stopped there. As for me, I see pulverization everywhere—as if reality is a woman cut up in a labyrinthine maze, and popping out whole at the end of the act is the illusion.

But there is the reverse, the mainstream: uncertainty as defense against desire and identity. We are confused because we are afraid to stand up and be counted, to be someone, afraid to form. Afraid to enter the sphere of the rival, where adults compete and play. Afraid to be real.

And here we are stuck: who says what is real? All the more pressing today when politicians say what reality is and political fiction defines the real. Bodies dying, as they often do, for definitions. Reality defined by power. To add a pinch of Freud to Marx: economic delusion driving reality.

Closer to my little world, the human psyche: one reason brain research gains the upper hand is because it claims a greater real, a greater promise, a greater deferral. There are chemical agents and neural spaces underwriting lust, love, and romance. Dopamine, norepinephrin for romance, testosterone for lust, oxytocin, vasopressin for attachment. Researchers watch brain images and decide what is more or less normal. Chemicals are developed to manipulate presumed imbalances for the better. Counter-reactions develop as unwanted side effects are discovered. Some chemicals make one less depressed but also less romantic. Some mood elevators or stabilizers mute, even obliterate, desire. There are antidepressants that make one feel more alive, jumpier, sometimes suicidal. Some individuals are happier on medication but also less aware of what others feel, not always a happy state of affairs.

A patient recently reported to me that his psychiatrist said, "This will make you feel better but diminish your libido." Look how casually the old term "libido" is used. I marveled at the easygoing acceptance of the puzzle. Little by little, chemical research will tease apart strands of feeling. Perhaps feeling bad or better and the pleasures of sex do not have to go together. Nevertheless, it's not for nothing that literature and history document intimate links between destruction and lust as well as the great heights passion achieves. Psychiatry has become almost carefree in saying, "Take this, it will make you feel better," without regard for the immense backdrop of knowledge poetry and politics provides. It is not unusual to walk out of a fifteen-minute psychiatric consultation with an array of heavy-duty medications addressing different complaints: one or two mood stabilizers, antidepressants, and something for anxiety. Chemical cocktails that have impressive results, enhancing quality of life, saving lives. Little by little, medications, we are promised, will cut down side effects like short-term memory loss and other cognitive difficulties, weight gain, sense of estrangement, drowsiness, fatigue, agitation, loss of contact with the subjective feelings of others, a subtle sense of estrangement, lack of ability to handle disturbing states on one's own, and other individual variations.

Researchers outline phases of lust and love and chemicals that go with them. Loss of interest, the need to regain the partner after letting go or being dumped, angry severance of the tie, withdrawal, depression fostering a further sense of reality. Any number of phases can be combined or deleted. There is the seducer who gets his joy of triumph, then runs away before undergoing the whole cycle of travail, the grim, growth-producing task of learning.

Now when one feels a lusty rush, one can say, that's my testosterone. Add a dash of falling in love and say, there goes my dopamine. Does this language add to the nuance and depth of experience or make us more facile? Both, at times?

Freud was raised on textbooks that located drives and emotions in the old brain, complex thinking in the new brain. Current research fills out the story, learning more about neural-chemical interaction and cortical/subcortical mapping. Flow and interweaving of neural processes are complex indeed. Pop dissemination of research enables many to seek help who otherwise might not. Nevertheless, one has to be careful not to support false ideas about difficulties we face. Even medicated people have to develop an ability to struggle, work with bad states, and discover what contribution one can make to enduring and bettering existence.

We may see what part of the brain lights up when we are attracted to someone, but we are not far enough along to reliably manipulate the site of attraction to our advantage or satisfaction, Viagra notwithstanding. People long have studied love potions to enhance pleasure or keep it from fading. In Shakespeare's *Midsummer Night's*

Dream, magic manipulates love chemistry, making people fall in or out of love according to a master will. Even this power over love finds obstacles that chance, fate, and human bungling must work through.

Pop psychology tends to reduce the complexity of our brain states *and* experience. Manipulating mood, image, and experience is big business, whether through print or video or pills. If one can squeeze experience into manageable boxes, control capability increases. However, much is lost by denuding experience of outside-the-box qualities. Increasingly, what is emphasized is how bits of experience can be turned to profit with the same attitude as pumping oil or depleting forests. I am unsure our capacity to experience is an un-limited resource able to survive brutal rip-off and toxic use. I believe at some point it requires care and that the capacity to care is itself in jeopardy. The *fullness of experience* may be one of the great, unrecog-nized endangered areas of life.

Let's pause a moment and appreciate a little of what we use, what we are given, what we find. For example, complexities of likes and dislikes. We like X, Y, and Z about a person, dislike E, F, and G. Some reactions hold up over time, others vary in a shake-and-mix way. We are sensitive to the smell and taste of each other's *psyches,* including tone or spirit or affective qualities. Yet we say we like Glo-ria, we hate Tom. The feel of a person makes up for a lot of sins or drowns out a lot of virtues. At the same time, our thinking about people grows by going back and forth, seeing someone in one light, then another.

We can be madly in love *and* give a scathing critique of the loved one. In one scenario, love and criticism evolve together, enriching the relationship, although not without difficulty. In another scenario, the mixture of love and judgment (the latter often aggressive, even hate-ful) is too incendiary, and the relationship explodes or dissolves. All mixes are possible, variation the rule. We spend a lifetime getting to know the equipment we've been given, what it offers, how to partner it. We need our capacity to idealize, to criticize, to intuit, feel, sense and think. For survival, certainly. But this term, "survival," deflects us from confessing something closer, more intimate, more real: how we feel to ourselves, how life feels. Survival takes us out of ourselves too quickly. It is useful up to a point, but turns into a quicksand concept, closing over the rich sense of what living is.

We train ourselves to ignore a good deal in our field of experience in favor of efficient functioning, goals, designs, or what we imagine to be useful schemes and fictions. For example, we try to localize weapons of mass destruction and destructive thoughts exterior to ourselves as if they are not somehow central to our beings. Weapons of mass destruction are scattered throughout the world, but *we* are the beings who made them. We like to see ourselves as designers and controllers, seekers of the good life, not destroyers. It is difficult to develop constructive relationships to the fact that destruction is intrinsic to our universe, and to us.

There are ways in which destruction feels good: we like to destroy. And the fact that lust often fuses with destructive urges ups the ante. The melding of destructive orgasms with the drive to win is part of the shocking euphoria of our day. To confess in our hearts that we are all weapons of mass or intimate destruction will not solve the massive problems that face us, but without a profound revision of attitude, we (the global community) don't stand a chance.

One pleasure adds to the sum of others and to the general enrichment of living. For example, reading, talking, walking, working and love-making add to life's bounties. There are times, though, when one capacity or another goes haywire and eats up the others. This is especially dramatic with regard to murder. Othello tries to blot out an inflammation (inflamed mind) by killing what he takes to be the offending object. Lust and murder and love devour each other, devour the object, devour the subject. The mocking heh-heh devil, here Iago, presses from host to host throughout history. It is a shock to discover that murder does not achieve the hoped-for result. Some who kill in war may taste destructive pleasures in the extreme, but many are injured by what they do, shaken by what murdering another can do to the self.

Dilemma: we may channel energy to destroy an enemy yet lose the feel of ourselves. Answer: if we don't destroy the enemy, we may not have a self to feel. Response: what if the enemy is suicidal behavior motored by delusion—religious and economic delusion that many further but no one so far knows how to stop (what? who me? I'm trying to help.)? What if suicide bombers are a visible index of a configuration more widely at work through other channels, for example, global economic mania that destroys the environment that supports life? Will the next great cataclysms be precipitated by economic mayhem, geopolitical rather than geological forces? What we are doing to ourselves as groups and individuals is the ice or heat age we most have to worry about now. Let's say the three words that are the depraved contemporary cross of the world: *lust for money*. The wealth of groups, individuals, nations: wealth can set you free. And there *is* a link between a modicum of wealth, freedom, and culture. The suicidal scenario changes, but the thrust is constant or accelerates. Since we are blessed with being a system of checks and balances, other capacities and ways of using ourselves may yet mitigate the fury of a warped, belligerent death lust (the undergradient of lust to be on top) that is busy at work, carving holes in dreams of glory.

It is not clear that widespread use of medication will solve such problems, even if we could legislate scientifically guided medication missiles for heads of state and diffuse infragroups. It is impossible to deduce complexity of experience from our knowledge of specific brain states. The fact that we can and do change experience by altering brain properties does not reduce the range of what we think and feel to the latter (not yet, although some are trying). Computers generate works of art and perhaps brain manipulation can too. But to generate a Shakespeare or Beethoven, you need a Shakespeare or Beethoven. This may apply to us psychic knit-pickers too, we who gravitate to bugs and scorpions of each other's insides and stick mental fingers and tongues into them. We are not happy with only the taste of sugar.

It does our capacity for research injury to ask the wrong things of it. Perhaps scientists will learn how to work with cortical/subcortical flow so people will not rape or kill. Sites for sex and mystical experience are close together. Perhaps hate and sex and love for God or a person or an image will get teased apart. What will we do with this power? Who will do it? What ethics of desire goes into composing a designer brain?

We insert electrodes deep in the brain to help people with behavioral disorders, just as we help the heart. Research money is given for physical approaches to experience. How experience affects experience is not marketable or perhaps is relegated to entertainment. At best, how experience affects the brain gets some attention (e.g., prolonged stress may alter brain chemistry and structure; to soothe another alters chemistry too). Thinking alters body states as well as the reverse. All fronts need work. All make contributions.

Therapy provides daily examples of intimacy between affective attitude and body life. Almost randomly, a few hours ago, a postmenopausal woman who lost sexual sensation, told me about rich and fulfilling sexual experiences with her husband. She was startled and pleased and attributed her opening to his change of attitude. "I felt he liked me," she said, "I opened and thawed." It happened by itself, feeling to feeling. She had long complained about his hostile impatience and had given up on sex. She had begun to accept being past the time: "Sex is gone, it left me," she often said.

Poets, feared to be an endangered species, proliferate among the young. Why? Don't they know studies show poets are sicker, more suicide prone than the general population and other artists? They are too sensitive, warped, outside the stream of things and can't help but give expression to whatever is wrong with their brains. Or is it that our brains need the special stimulation poetry brings, that nothing quite substitutes for this way of opening reality and enlarging experience? Poetry is part of what we do to preserve, foster, nourish quality of experiencing. Poetry is part of caring for the possibilities of experience. This caring is at risk, and we need those who would shepherd it.

There is an X that defies marketability as a criterion of worth, a need for quality of expression. A way to employ hallucination without mass murder. Sense life for its own sake. See what language can do.

Experience gets ahead of the brain, and the latter must rush to catch up. A bit like stepping off a cliff over an abyss, challenging evolution to provide a net. There is a need to squeeze past what the brain can do, then give the latter time to find a new point of entry.

Spring, Summer, Autumn, Winter . . . Spring Again—a German/Korean movie, is not your usual coming-of-age movie, yet it is all too, too usual, that is, real. A beautiful boy is raised by a Buddhist monk who instills his charge with a profound feel for life. The boy grows, and a young woman is brought to their houseboat, which floats with life of its own on a pond in the midst of beauty, surrounded by woods, mountains, sky.

The girl is ill, but little by little her health returns, achieved fully by sexual realization. We see the young couple copulating in the midst of nature. The young man expresses shame, guilt, but that does not stop nature from taking its course. It is an Asian version of Freud's prescription for hysteria.

It's time for the cured young woman to leave, and the young man can't bear parting from her. He takes off after her, marries her; time passes, and we learn of her murder. Our once-innnocent young man, enthralled by erotic bliss, killed his wife in a fit of jealousy. We see him as emotionally contracted, unrecognizable, torn and corrupted by the world. He could not bear his beloved's infidelity. All this was predicted by the master earlier: "Lust leads to possession, possession to murder." His young charge had to find out for himself.

There were trials as a child, trials as an adult. As a child, he tied rocks to small creatures—a fish, a snake, a frog—and laughed at their difficulty, the force that worked against mobility. His master told him to free the animals, for if they died, they would be stones in his heart for the rest of his life. Two died, and the boy wept uncontrollably, meeting the pain that rips us apart, inconsolable pain. How can such agony exist?

He met the pain again when his beloved left and again after he killed her.

After serving his prison term, he returns to the houseboat, his master gone by an act of self-immolation, clearing the way. It is now the chastened man's time to master himself, and we witness his self-training. When he is ready, an unknown mother brings him a child to care for. She drowns as she walks back across the icy pond toward land. In another act of expiation and transformation, he ties a heavy stone to his waist and stumbles up a mountain, where he places a Buddha on the stone, atop the world, to protect the world.

Cruelty, lust, murder, birth, death—as natural as beauty. And the drive toward transcendence? Also natural? Self-giving, the need to help and be helped, squeezed out of the agony, a caring core.

An inside-out movement: lust expresses love, love transcends lust, lust drives transcendence. What kind of transcendence? A cruel or loving kind? A caring or cut-off need for a larger horizon? Lust burrows from an untraceable place deep inside the frame. It burrows from one horizon to another. A burrowing that is also a catapulting, a leaping, a firing of a weapon.

A worm hole is one kind of lust, a locomotive another. To go in one place, come out another far, far away. To persist, to drive, unwavering until the destination comes.

Lust is associated with lower levels of life, with being asleep to our higher nature. Lust wakes us, makes us realize there is more.

"I am most alive sexually when I don't love."
"I am most alive sexually when I love."
Many say both.

Is it hard to admit that pleasure is fused with everything else, with pain?
To say so is an act of cruelty.
There is no end to pleasure in cruelty, especially the cruelty that rejects the fact that there *is* such a thing as agony without pleasure.

Lust, nearly as repetitive as breathing, takes us to new places, affirms, makes life alive, creates eternal moments.
We will not speak here about the drop, fall, loss, undoing, collapse, food for the vortex. This sentence is dedicated to the scent of affirmation.

Lust generates.
Lust destroys.
Lust is predatory.
Lust is delicious.
Lust is our skin and glands and muscles and sensory organs.
Lust is fantasy, hallucination, delusion.

Lust breaks through reality.

Lust opens reality.

Lust fuses with everything: power, fame, enlightenment, great works, a hunger for the real, the true, the beautiful. Lust for writing, lust for art. Fame is a decoy, a lure, a spur—not the original impulse. A trick, like sex, to get us into creativity with all its risks.

And lust for writing, this writing, this word? Writing is the art of making false statements ring true. Not only ring true: bear truth, bare truth. Writing as a readying for truth.

Writing, the kind I'm talking about, gets ahead of, underneath, or to the side of the brain, and the brain has to keep up with it. Writing takes the brain, like a pet, out for a walk. Without much of a leash. Not much to hold on to.

If one looked too closely, it would be even scarier than it feels. It is possible that writing will take the brain to a place where the link between them will be lost. This is one meaning of tales that express fear of not finding one's way back.

Lust that is less in words and more in organs has an easier time finding its way back to the body it burns through, but not finding its way to the other home writing discovers. Writing straddles soul dimensions, and that may seem reassuring, but it is less scary to stay behind.

Moebius strip, on the one hand, split on the other. On the floor clutching oneself, pasting oneself together. Many people roll on the floor (or want to), clutching their agony. A nonspecific agony existence brings. It is hard to remember and hold on to lust's ecstasy at such a time. The term "bipolar" has been misappropriated by psychiatry. "Bipolar" is a beautiful term. A person gripped by extreme swings that destroys her life is one thing. But the fact that we are a being made up of extreme emotions is another.

To make contact with another's body is enough.

To make contact with another's body is not enough.

To turn inside out: flesh ↔ spirit. Look how we try. Words like insects rushing toward fire. I want to see where light comes from. I know it is inside bodies.

I think that is why we dissect ourselves, to find the source of Light.

Radiance of genitals in every pore. Every cell a climax.

Lust obliterates the face.

Lust awakens the face.

Face encircles lust, horizons within horizons.

"I saw a baby drink in soul from her mother's eyes," a patient tells me about watching a baby nurse this weekend. "My soul glanced off my mother's eyes. Her eyes were wounding like a weapon."

The beauty of the first image, the pain of the second spread through the room.

The pain of deflected soul, turned away by eyes of sharp glass, bleeding heart indeed! Or soul fading, ossifying in vacant eyes. "I became a vampire to escape my bloody cuts. To escape my disappearance. I fill myself with blood to wipe out the basic fault."

No matter how much sex, not enough. Sex works overtime, filling cuts and vacancies. Sex gives hate a home. "What drives blood lust? Not enough soul from a mother's eyes."

The human face provides a home for faceless lust. Lust drives toward facelessness, toward homelessness.

She sits, looks, smiles in an awful way: "I'm good at blood lust. I'm a good vampire. I'll suck all the blood out of this analysis and still not be me. I can't be me. All the blood-drinking. Bloodbaths. All the blood in the world won't wash away the basic fault."

Yet sex makes her feel good. Lust brings a taste of happiness.

~~~ I don't believe that death succeeds in eating lust.

I do believe that lust succeeds in eating death.

This does not deny that lust brings death into the world and death intensifies lust. They unleash each other.

One could as easily say lust and death disappear each other, if ecstatic and grisly realities didn't trail in their wake.

Credit domains.

~~~ When lust and death eat each other—where does the face go?

Disappearance is uneven.

~~~ One can lose the face of the other as an organizing frame and try to pitch battle in other domains. For example, a recovering schizophrenic woman: "Eat is part of death. Ear is part of hear. Eat is part of heat. I got ear infections before I was a year from my mother's inability to hear. She couldn't let me in. She felt me by plunging into me. The sound of her plunged into me. I tried to shut her sound out. Hearing terrified me. I shut her out so much I feared going deaf. I am excruciatingly sensitive. Breathe on me and I come. Yet I shut life out. I am deaf. You penetrate me all over. You spread through me like liquid. I shut you out. My body is an ear that doesn't hear. They say you can't keep sound out: you can, you *can*." In her case, vision was eclipsed by a battle with sound, scarred and dissolved by conflict over hearing. To hear or not to hear became everything. Hearing can eat you up, spread everywhere, unmodulated by vision. In such a case, sound leaves boundless holes.

"When I was young I didn't know how to go deaf. I didn't know how to make it [everything, life, self, bad stuff, maternal impinge-ment, infiltration] go away and [self, life, good stuff] still be there. I got ear infections. I created other ears. I created an ear below, in my underneath. This is real, taking in from below, through my under-neath secret insides. All through childhood my vagina was a secret ear and no one knew, my *real* ear. I knew people *that* way, a secret taking. Quite a fix. I had a sexual sensor. Sexual heat, my way to eat. Once in me, it [whatever, world, self, sound, threat] disappears. You come in and disappear. You dissolve. Sound dissolves in sex without a trace. Hidden sex. I used to fear getting pregnant doing this but nothing ever got born."

This woman nearly mastered the art of looking as if she were there. She keeps her eyes open for long periods without blinking so that she would look as if she were seeing. She mimicked having eyes so people would see her and think she was there. In fact, there were no faces, only blank stares. She turned others into blanks, while se-cretly supping from below. No visual brakes for sound bites. One of the great contributions of therapy: no matter how much we disap-pear, we meet again. It is one thing to meet a world that does not know it is not there, something else to meet a being for whom disap-pearance is natural, part of the rise and fall of breathing.

The disturbance of lust. Someone dreams of rubbing her face clean, rubbing, rubbing. Rubbing soul clean of the scandal of distur-bance. Robbing it of life.

One more rub and a genie will appear with more disruptive wishes.

A woman confides that waking up is a kind of climax.

Another woman tells me, "At the age of twenty, I woke up to pain." This is what literature tries and almost fails to tell us. The quake of pain, taboo truth, that agony is necessary.

Lust creates the illusion that agony is unnecessary. Lust promises to circumvent agony. It promises wonder, awe, amazing experience. "Great sex," is a popular phrase, in keeping with our lust for greatness, our belief that anything less is a failure.

And the worlds lust opens to the unsuspecting? To the artist of lust?

🖋 Sadistic lust trades on another's agony. It wears the other as a mask. Secretly insinuates itself inside the other's body, puts on the other's body. It needs the other's pain as antidote, as supplement to one's own.

Loving lust inflicts pleasure, not pain. A generous whipping-up of pleasure, bliss. Thrill fills the universe, no room for horror, yet. Incite, excite is all.

Generous lust is amazed when horror comes. How could it expect such collapse of bliss? Pain was left behind. Only the goodness of a delicious force was real *and* hoped to be real.

But agony does come, and generosity does not understand it. A child's fingers toward a flame: how can beauty burn?

A burning that is the initiate's daily trade.

Does sadistic lust laugh last?

🖋 Cruelty, generosity: lust a battleground.

🖋 A wise man said, "Sex is a place you can be as aggressive as you want and it comes out good. The more you pour yourself into, against the other, the better." A variant of his saying, "Sex is one of those places where aggression creates, adds to pleasure, a place where aggression doesn't harm." To be aggressive without injury—one of the great benefits of sex. Of course, you have to place these sayings in the right light to set them free.

≈ Generative lust.

Destructive lust.

What do we do with destructiveness? Akin to what do we do with love?

≈ Lust for beginnings? Quality of approach? Issues of attitude and feeling?

Security has shaky, wobbly components.

≈ Creativity without passion? Without creativity lust?

≈ A lot of passion goes into being dispassionate.

≈ Passion is a bad word: we speak of emptying ourselves of passion.

Passion is a good word: we speak of our passion for this, passion for that, as if passion confers value on ourselves and life.

Passion as badge or drive. Something to overcome, channel, transform. Something to be transformed by. Something to use and be used by. Show off with, take off with, reach heaven or hell with. One of the world's great wonders. An amazement.

A good in itself, adding life to life, making life *life*.

≈ Lust drives us toward others. Others excite. We want them, go after them, take them, absorb them, dip in repeatedly. No end to more.

Freud's genius: it is already there, the way the nipple feels to the mouth, in the mouth, the liquid, the hardening and softening, skin on skin, naked mouth everywhere.

In the light, the eyes, the face, the arms. Deliciousness of form and color, of expression and expressiveness.

A cosmic vision, as Hindus saw, a male-female universe, interlocking inside-outside each other, a libidinous universe stretching toward symbolic sentience.

⟡ Too bad lust destroys. Others strewn in its wake, discarded. Civilizations wiped out. Life's incessant query: how can something so good be so bad? Life puzzled by itself?

Lust reaches beyond itself, hurls us past ourselves. We spend a lot of time playing catch up without knowing it, a silly game with monstrous consequences. There's no getting away from it. The great process of fecundity. Many plunge in, others try to get around it. Some try to wait.

⟡ Selfish lust stops cold at the wall of the other. It fails to penetrate, take hold, grab hold. There is no renewal because there are no insides—no resonant insides. It falls off the wall of the other back to the self, lost in self. Self is enough. Self is all. There is no other, just excitement, the act. The other as fantasy, as pleasure, part of my will.

The first act the last. Always the end. One-way feed—all done! A pleasure feed for one, others pay in pain. Pain pays for pleasure. A selfish lust that costs, that humanity pays for. *We* pay the price for a willfully driven I.

Different from mutual selfishness—always beginning, a pleasure pool. A fresh try.

⟡ A fresh try to get inside each other, find each other there.

⟡ Perhaps reaching beyond is the point. Lust drives us beyond.

Perhaps lust's not caring what it does to us is the point. Lust doesn't care about death in childbirth, jealous deaths, creating and destroying families. It cares only about itself. But ever leads elsewhere.

Lust gets us out of ourselves (whether for longer or shorter times). A man, used to retreating to sanatoriums, was blessed enough to be able to follow the trajectory of an impulse awakened by a nurse and tasted what Freud called, a "breakthrough to the woman."

A breakthrough to life's bounty, riddled with difficulties. To break through to the other puts self and other at risk. Loss becomes possible. This is different from the selfish lust in which there is no loss. Where self and other are at risk, loss is part of pleasure. New domains of injury swim into view. Renewal and possibility become real, relevant. Living achieves new stature.

Diotima teaches Socrates that eros is a vehicle, an opening to the Vision of the Good, a stepping stone. Could we reach the Good without it?

As if lust ignites mind or spirit, starts a flame that does not end, smolders and ascends, discovers what is possible.

And the fistlike quality of possessive lust, bending life to itself, gripping it, contracting it to what a smaller ego can encompass?

What would we look like if we disentangled lust from murder? Is that even possible?

Let's give Freud the last or next-to-last word. Lust always is doing something. No one is above it. It reaches beyond the grave of self, long after dying out. It lives in fantasy, in politics, in power, in the way one human being relates to another, in possessiveness, in caring. It is, indeed, what ethics is about. It is, in part, why Cain killed Abel and brothers of the human race go on killing to this day.

Can lust and respect exist in the same universe? The challenge is that they do. Kant was mystified: where does *ought* come from? The desire, the need, the obligation to do right by life, to do life justice. It seems at odds with lust and power and the rule of mutual antagonisms. Kant does not settle for this guiding star—this great "commandment"—as a mere practical convenience. In his vision, it is what nature and evolution are all about, a grand teleology, leading to the rule of duty, of respect and caring, doing right by each other. Or, in his great formulation, treating one another as ends, not merely as means.

We cannot fault Kant for being unrealistic. He sees life's cruelties and pleasures as they are. He wonders where this excess comes from, the drive to do good, to be just? Is it the goal of all our strivings, the goal of history? He does not say it is realizable in fact, but as a "guiding thread" helps draw life a little more toward respect and care for who we are, what we have been given, what we can do. He does seem to feel that now it is up to us and that, paradoxically, this being up to us is part of nature's plan or providence.

What can respect for lust mean? I think we need to find out.

Perhaps as a minimum we can say that respect and lust are parts of a greater system (sets of systems) of checks and balances. We can begin by saying that, for now, there is no solution to the diversity of tensions, lust and human rights, lust and caring. To take the notion of partners further, what can partnering our capacities mean? We cannot solve or dis-solve our tensions, but we *can* grow and develop by working with them.

We do not want to be caring, respectful ciphers. Perhaps the human race is a bit like the protagonist in *Equus*, afraid it will lose its vitality, color, and aliveness if it solves its neurosis-psychosis or becomes too peaceful. Perhaps one resists change because one is afraid to lose the aliveness one has, the realness one knows. And perhaps this sometimes is a real danger.

There are stories and movies that portray the enlightened being of the future (often extraterrestrial) as nearly pure heads, rational minds with little need for bodies. It is one attempt to portray a lust-free universe, not a very likely outcome for most of us. There seems to lurk fear and interest in the possibility that one of our capacities or another will win a lopsided battle. We point to lust's tragedies as reason to be reasonable. We point to overmentalization as reason to be lustful. In both cases, tension between capacities is skirted and the growth that comes from struggle with tensions is shunted.

Kant's description of the moral universe as more beautiful than the starry skies is thrilling for some, chilling for others. For me, his words, his thought, his vision send chills up and down my spine—thrilling chills. Lust, in the background, informs it, for the moment dissolves into it. A thrill of victory of what is good in the human heart, of what is highest in human nature.

Such a thought gains power, partly, because we feel beneath or behind it what we cannot—may never be able to—surmount. There is no antidote to lust as disturbance except in wishful thinking. Disturbance changes forms. There is no solution to the challenges our makeup poses. But, as I said, we grow through working with the raw materials that make us up. And the respectful, caring attitude expressed by Kant lends fervor to our work. To treat each other, all life, the cosmos as ends means there is no end to beginnings. Lust sees to that.

Afterword

We are still evolving and *need* to evolve. What we call lust is evolving with us and we with it. Evolution is uneven. There are many ways to relate to lust, to link with it, and, as we evolve, more and more depends on *quality* of approach. How we approach an experience has an enormous influence on the experience itself. Experience is, partly, a labor. We help midwife the birth of experience. The way we touch and taste ourselves plays an important role in what sorts of birth we undergo. Experience is the true garden we are asked to tend. The Garden of Eden story depicts the birth of suffering, a movement to fuller or different experience. Lust plays a role in this awakening, this arousal, like a horn calling us into life. It's no accident that "horns" once suggested sexual jealousy and betrayal and today means "horny" (sexually itchy).

For some, horn is too phallic, even though air goes through its opening, like breath, sensation, through the reed of the body. Let the horn dissolve. Let there be only tissue tingling. Let that be our consciousness for the moment, a tingling consciousness. Whether loud blasts or soft spreads, we know something is going on. Something is happening. Perhaps lust takes us away from larger life by narrowing the band of interest. Perhaps it opens what is possible by intensifying points of contact. One moment we run toward it, another moment away. It spreads and flows toward and away with a life of its own. We are at a loss, bend low and wait. We hear the wind, feel it. We wait for more. We wish there weren't so many people telling us what life is or isn't. It is better to discover how to speak with life ourselves.

Notes and References

p. 1: "The human being has always . . .": J. Lacan (1978), *The Four Fundamental Concepts of Psycho-Analysis*, ed. Jacques-Alain Miller, trans. A. Sheridan, New York: W. W. Norton, p. 204.

p. 6: "Primal words": S. Freud (1910), "Antithetical Meaning of Primal Words," *Standard Edition*, 11:255.

p. 9: Jacob's land purchase parallels his grandfather Abraham's land purchases. The grisly tale about Dinah, Shechem, and her brothers (Jacob's sons) unfolds in Genesis 34. The stories of Abraham's land purchases are in Genesis 21, 23. Leaving and returning is a theme that stamps the Bible, from beginning to end. There are many meanings of exile-return, including physical, geopolitical, emotional. It is expressed in early infancy (mother leaving-returning, self waxing-waning, peek-a-boo, full and empty feelings related to feeding), in childhood games (hide and seek), getting together and breaking up in relationships, loss and refinding of self in growth experiences and life stages, inner states of coming together–falling apart, the hovering specter of loss of life in contrast with being alive now. Going and coming in physical and emotional terms has a parallel in the rise and fall of sexual feeling, tumescence-detumescence.

p. 9: Adam and Eve hear God's voice walking: Genesis 3. Here God's presence takes the form of voice. One way of thinking about it is that this is God's voice as the background hum of silence in the universe, made audible in tensions between pleasure and shame, limit and transgression. What is expressed is a going beyond, an inability to remain confined or to remain where one is. The discomfort Adam and Eve feel has to do with the urgency of transcendence, not being able to stay in one place inwardly, owing to the life of the image ("made in God's image"), the movement of thought. They hide their nakedness because, in fact, simple nakedness is no longer possible for the dreadful, thrilling flash of mind.

p. 13: Jacob's death and final blessings and prophesies, his acute appraisal of his sons and their destinies: Genesis 49.

p. 14: E. Abbott (1884), *Flatland: A Romance of Many Dimensions*, London: Penguin Classics, 1998.

p. 15: Face-to-face vision: Moses has a personal relationship with God, hears and sees God, a relationship that ultimately melds with providing laws to live by. Moses' credentials as having a direct connection with God are established in Exodus. Three books of law and adventure follow (Leviticus, Numbers, Deuteronomy), in which personal God-connection melds with law-giving, turning a tribe into a potential godly nation. While laws seek to regulate lust, there is a clear connection between lust and violence, and it is, above all, destructiveness the Bible seeks to regulate. However, it often does this in destructive ways. Freud gives voice to fusions of desire and aggression in his concept of libido. He has many passages linking religious idealization to guilt over destructiveness, the latter partly fueled by lust (e.g., "Totem and Taboo" [1913], *Standard Edition*, 14; 1939, and "Moses, His People, and the Monotheist Religion" [1939], *Standard Edition*, 23). Neither religion nor sex can be a solution to destructiveness since, for Freud, the life drive has destructive elements.

p. 15: a destructive cleansing after the sin of the golden calf: Exodus 32:25–35.

p. 22: Freud's "rat man": A case Freud analyzed in which a symptom was dread of rats penetrating the anus. This portrayal includes great pages on magical thinking. S. Freud (1909), "Notes upon a Case of Obsessional Neurosis," *Standard Edition*, 10.

p. 24: desire itself as plenitude, a fullness, richness of life: For a heartening affirmation of positive aspects of desire, see Mark Epstein (2005) *Open to Desire: Embracing a Lust for Life Insights from Buddhism and Psychotherapy*. New York: Gotham Press. See also *Toxic Nourishment* (1999), London: Karnac Books, chap. 12, "Desire and Nourishment."

p. 25: *Katha Upanishad.*

p. 25: Donald Hall (2002), "Villanelle", *The Painted Bed*, Boston: Houghton Mifflin, p. 83. "Villanelle" is one of a series of sexual poems in *The Painted Bed*, a book growing out of the death of Hall's wife, Jane. It is in the last section of the book, the section entitled "Charity and Dominion," which follows a brief section called "Ardor." The first two sections, more than half the book, are called "Kill the Day" and "Deathwork," titles that capture the concern and mood of these poems. We walk with the poet with his grief and his memories to places he and Jane touched and to a place where nothing touches her body but earth. The final section is like a bursting of spring, tempered by winter clinging to our guts. The poet takes us to Jane's grave, before taking us to their bed.

p. 26: to lose everything: ". . . it is fitting / and delicious to lose everything" ("Affirmation", ibid., p. 87).

p. 28: "A thing of beauty . . .": Keats, "Endymion."

p. 28: "Green grape, no go . . .": A loose remembering of something I read in the Greek anthology fifty years ago. I looked it up to discover what memory loses:

> Green grape, and you refused me.
>
> Ripe grape, and you sent me packing.
>
> Must you deny me a bite of your raisin?

Poems from the Greek Anthology (1956), trans. Dudley Fitts, New York: New Directions, p. 49.

p. 30–31: "when the lips and the skin remember . . .": "The Return" in *The Complete Poems of Cavafy* (1989), trans. Rae Dalven, New York: Harcourt, p. 43; "Enjoyment of the flesh . . .": "To Remain," ibid., p. 94. "Comes to Rest," in C. P. Cavafy (1992), *Collected Poems*, ed. G. Savidis, trans. Edmund Keeley and Philip Sherrard, Princeton: Princeton University Press, p. 97.

p. 31: "my whole being radiating . . .": I've somewhat rephrased these lines from "Outside the House" in Cavafy, *Collected Poems*, p. 94. The poet passes by a house of love he frequented as a youth, suddenly the old road, "the shops, the sidewalks, the stones, / walls and balconies and windows . . . all made beautiful by the spell of love."

p. 32: "Body, remember . . .": "Body, Remember," Cavafy, ibid., p. 84.

p. 34: "whose characteristic is not to exist": "This lamella, this organ, whose characteristic is not to exist, but which is nevertheless an organ—I can give you more details as to its zoological place—it is the libido." Lacan, *The Four Fundamental Concepts of Psycho-Analysis*, pp. 197–98.

p. 34: "It is the libido, *qua* pure life instinct . . .": ibid.

p. 35: "ungraspable organ," "false organ": ibid., p. 196.

p. 36–37: "The libido is the essential organ . . .": ibid., p. 205.

p. 55: Lilith, in legend Adam's first wife, a particularly strong demon. See Isaac Bashevis Singer, *The Magician of Lublin*, for an example of her powers. Lacan has passages that express a sense of being suffocated by ourselves, our need to get out of ourselves. "The subject is subject only by being subjected to the field of the Other. . . . That is why he must get out, get himself out, and in the *getting-himself-out*, in the end, he will know that the real Other has, just as much as himself, to get himself out, to pull himself free." (ibid., p. 188) A kind of fading or dying out is part of the admission price for being a symbolizing being ("What the subject has to free himself of is the aphanisic effect of the binary signifier," ibid., p. 219). One tears at the fading and the dying that afflicts a meaning-making being. Lily leaves staring through a glass darkly at the great mystery of love beneath a screen of stabs and suffocation inflicted by snakes of affect and meaning, a great love which in the human sphere is marked by grave limitations (including all the wounds and scars of living). Lust tries to blast through aphanisis, to get out. Lust tries to blast through trauma. In Lily's case it almost worked in conjunction with other capacities like brain power. But caring came and with that, a more complex puzzle.

p. 55: Marriage brought such conflict for Lily, going against what seemed natural for her. Perhaps the price she paid for love was too great. She had to twist herself out of shape, go through agonies. She might have been better off without it. Can one know?

p. 55: Aphanisis: fading, dying, as in the deadness that is part of being a signifying being (see first note for p. 55; Lacan, *The Four Fundamental Concepts of Psycho-Analysis*, chap. 17, "The Subject and the Other: Aphanisis").

p. 59: Garden of Eden: Genesis 1–3: I've written about a "heh-heh" devil mocking experience in *The Psychotic Core* (1986), London: Karnac Books. For more on demonized aspects of the self, see *The Electrified Tightrope*, (1993), ed. A. Phillips, London: Karnac Books, chap. 16.

p. 61: distinction-union structure and depictions of the birth of the self: *The Psychotic Core*, chap. 4; *Reshaping the Self* (1995), Madison, Conn.: Psychosocial Press.

p. 62: S. Freud (1914), "On Narcissism: An Introduction," *Standard Edition*,

14:73–102. Wilhelm Reich's work is rich with depictions of sensory spreads we defend against, so much so that he speaks of character as armor against sensation fields. W. Reich (1949), *Character Analysis*. New York: Farrar, Straus & Cudahy. Norman O. Brown (1959), *Life Against Death: A Psychoanalytic Meaning of History*. Middletown, Conn.: Wesleyan University Press) wrote of the resurrection of the body as reclaiming the life of the senses, as did a swelling chorus of voices in the 1960s (e.g., E. Straus [1963], *The Primary World of the Senses*, London: The Free Press of Glencoe).

p. 62: poetry quotations from William Blake's *The Marriage of Heaven and Hell*.

p. 63: "Man has no Body distinct from his Soul . . .": ibid.

p. 64: To turn a heart of stone into a heart of flesh is a recurrent prophetic call, "circumcision of the heart." Sometimes lust does this, sometimes it does the opposite, allied with cruelty. One woman told me, "Lust melts the metal band around my heart." For her, being with a baby did this even more. A link between pleasure, fecundity, and the delicious thrill new life brings. An opening deeper than any organ.

p. 64: difficulties on the path to lust: For representative texts on complexities, currents, cross- and counter-currents, multilayering, multidimensions of drives in psychoanalysis: S. Freud, (1915), "Instincts and Their Vicissitudes," *Standard Edition*, 14; (1905), "Three Essays on the Theory of Sexuality" *Standard Edition*, 7; (1910), "Leonardo Da Vinci and a Memory of His Childhood, *Standard Edition*, 11. Lacan, *The Four Fundamental Concepts of Psycho-Analysis*, chaps. 12–15. Lacan drives his logic as far as possible, not just asserting that there are *only* partial drives (no such thing as a "whole" or single drive—all drives are made up of subdrives and crosscurrents), but going so far as to declare, outrageously, that the genital drive is located nowhere. The non-sense of this drives us to more thoroughly and profoundly reflect on what sort of psychic makeup we have and the role the unconscious subject plays in constituting what we call sexuality (see p. 34 and the first note for it).

p. 64: that the whole sexual drive is located nowhere: Lacan, *The Four Fundamental Concepts of Psycho-Analysis*, p. 189. See above, p. 34

p. 66: Freud's daughter's dream of food: ibid., p. 155; "Impulse is satisfied essentially by hallucination": ibid., p. 154.

p. 67: "It is only on account of the sexualization . . .": ibid., p. 155.

p. 67–68: drive as a constant force: ibid., p. 164; "In the subject who, alternately, reveals himself . . .": ibid., p. 188.

p. 69: reversible figure-ground, beauty-hag: Gestalt psychology demonstrated the importance of whole-object and form perception, parts being immediately seen as parts of larger wholes. Perceptions of wholes do not have to be filtered through meta-levels of representations and judgments but spontaneously constitute themselves. One illustration of oscillating figure-ground is an image that one moment looks like a beautiful woman, the next moment like a hag. The theory involved transient saturation of aspects of brain fields connected with shifts in perceptual organization (e.g., K. Koffka [1935], *Principles of Gestalt Psychology*, New York: Harcourt, Brace).

p. 70: "to the circulation of the Oedipus complex": Lacan, *The Four Fundamental Concepts of Psycho-Analysis*, p. 189; drive as montage: ibid., p. 176.

p. 70–71: "The *ganze Sexualstrebung* is nowhere . . .": ibid., p. 189; "The subject as such is uncertain because . . .": ibid., p. 188.

p. 71: To desire the desire of the other is a complex theme of Lacan's, with many layerings. The phrase, "desire of the Other," traverses the influence of the other's desire on my desire, my own inner desire of the Other, our desire to desire, the Other's desire as obstacle to fading constituted through fading (presence-absence or appearance-disappearance as a given of subjectivity/intersubjectivity), the subject's recognition of desire as desire of the other (e.g., ibid., p. 235: "Man's desire is the desire of the Other"). Lacan calls this relation internal. It may be that he means internal to the subject. I feel it is important to realize a kind of immediacy in this mediate relation, a link, resonance, an immediate tug or contact of desire to desire (or its lack), a subject-subject relation, inner to inner (see *The Psychotic Core*, chap. 4). Desire connects with desire or its negative. It is instantaneous, although it may take other psychic systems time to catch up and catch on. That it is instantaneous does not mean specifics of content do not change. But the vibratory structure of desire-to-desire (or its lack) is a constant. Lacan encompasses the desire not to desire as part of this nexus in his image of a "Moebius strip that has no underside" (ibid.)

p. 74: "The living being . . .": ibid., p. 205; "the essential affinity . . .": ibid., p. 199.

p. 74: Saint Augustine, *Confessions*.

p. 75: death's fusion with pleasure (e.g., bloodlust): For portrayals of death-destructiveness/*jouissance*/ecstasy fusions, see *Ecstasy* (2001), Middletown, Conn.: Wesleyan University Press.

p. 76: the unreal: Lacan, *The Four Fundamental Concepts of Psycho-Analysis*, pp. 197–99, 205–8; above, pp. 33–38, 64, 70–71, 75.

p. 76: "The breast—as equivocal . . .": ibid., p. 198.

p. 79: "When the subject appears somewhere . . .": ibid., p. 218.

p. 79: "I am another": Rimbaud's *voyat* letters (1871). Whitman's "I am multitudes" appeared in 1855 (*Leaves of Grass*). Rimbaud was very taken with Baudelaire's, *Fleurs du Mal*, published in 1857. See *The Psychotic Core*, chaps. 1, 6.

p. 79: aphanisis: Lacan, *The Four Fundamental Concepts of Psycho-Analysis*, chap.17. See also pp. 57 and 112.

p. 80: to try to free oneself from aphanisis: ibid., p. 219.

p. 81: The disappearing subject and aphanisis: ibid., chaps. 16 and 17; Gary and Marge: above, pp. 76–79.

p. 82: Such a term, "cracked up," combining slit, lip, breakage, chance, luck, laughter, madness, and slight opening of a secret.

p. 83: *The Complete Letters of Sigmund Freud to Wilhelm Fliess, 1887–1904*, trans. and ed. J. M. Masson, Cambridge: Harvard University Press, 1985. Freud's essay on Leonardo also suggests the role bisexual currents play in creative work (see second note for p. 64).

p. 83–84: Marie Coleman Nelson's remark comes from a seminar I took with her and personal conversation in 1974.

p. 84–85: addition and reproduction: see W. R. Bion (1992), *Cogitations*, London: Karnac Books, p. 145. Links between numbers and various dimensions of meaning are ancient. Counting warriors: In the Bible, Numbers starts with a head count of men useable for battle. There is a story that God enjoyed counting Hebrews as a rich man counts his money or jewels (valuables, precious). To be counted also means to count, to be worth something.

p. 85: psychic monogamy-monotheism, the ego as unifier of sensory-emotive flow: Freud, "On Narcissism" (see first note for p. 62). For the breaking apart–recovering rhythm, see *The Sensitive Self* (2004), Middletown, Conn.: Wesleyan University Press, chap. 2, and *Coming Through the Whirlwind* (1992), Wilmette, Ill.: Chiron Publications, chaps. 1 and 2.

p. 86: every storm: *Emotional Storm* (2205), Middletown, Conn.: Wesleyan University Press (2005).

p. 87: I used to joke that Jews have more names for God than Eskimos Have for snow. Plural names for the singular God (hidden polytheism: gods find refuge in God's names?), but also a singular name for plurality associated with God. In the saying, "Hear O Israel, the Lord [*Adoshem*] is God [*Elokenu*], God [*Adoshem*] is One," or "Hear O Israel, the Lord [*Adoshem*] our God [*Elokenu*], the Lord [*Adoshem*] is One," or similar variants: *Elokenu* is the plural aspect of God, *Adoshem*, the unity or singular or oneness aspect. Something like Freud's narcissistic ego unifying sensory-affective streaming ("On Narcissism"). Mystical religion may speak of plurality-unity of souls or soul with God. For psychic pulverization, see *The Sensitive Self*, chap. 3; for the plural I, see *The Psychotic Core*.

pp. 88–89: Lust may be supported or driven by testosterone in both sexes, romantic love with dopamine and norepinephrine, attachment with oxytocin and vasopressin. For a popular treatment, see H. Fisher (2004), *Why We Love: The Nature and Chemistry of Romantic Love*, New York: Henry Holt. See also A. Janov (2000), *The Biology of Love*, Amherst, N.Y.: Prometheus Books. In complex symbolic creatures (ourselves) we should keep in mind that meaning triggers chemistry, including the chemistry of attraction. Attraction has meaning and is evoked by meaning and does not result only from blind chemical triggers.

Many factors affect brain chemistry, including abuse, separation from loved ones, stress, and severe isolation. Positive experiences affect chemistry too. For a review of studies that show brain changes linked to psychotherapy, see M. Beutel, E. Stern, and D. Silbersweig (2003), *Journal of the American Psychoanalytic Association* 51:773–801. For a summary of the propinquity of sex, rage, and mystical experience brain "areas," see R. Joseph (1996), *Neuropsychiatry, Neuropsychology, and Clinical Neuroscience*, Baltimore, Md.: Williams and Wilkins. The website of the International Society for the Psychological Treatments of the Schizophrenias and Other Psychoses emphasizes the importance of psychological factors in brain/experience interweaving (www.isps.org).

p. 92: inner and outer checks and balances: We are made up of a multitude of capacities that check and balance each other, e.g., thinking-feeling, hallucinating-reflecting, mythopoetic intuition–analytic thinking, and so on. To divide legislative, administrative, judicial functions in governance is an evolutionary attempt to express aspects of our nervous system externally in potentially useful ways. Adaptive plasticity reshapes notions of stability.

p. 94: poets and mental illness and early death: J. C. Kaufman (2003), "The Cost of the Muse: Poets Die Young," *Death Studies*, 27(9):813–22; (2001), "The Sylvia Plath Effect: Mental Illness in Eminent Creative Writers, *The Journal of Creative Behavior*, 35(1):37–50; A. M. Ludwig (1995), *The Price of Greatness: Resolving the Creativity and Madness Controversy*, New York: Guilford.

p. 96: The possibility of agony without pleasure is approached in *Psychic Deadness* (1996), London: Karnac Books; *Toxic Nourishment*; and *Damaged Bonds* (2002), London: Karnac Books. One of the most dramatic formulations of pure destruction is Bion's force that goes on working after it destroys everything, destruction that feeds on destruction when nothing is left (W. R. Bion [1965], *Transformations*, London: Karnac Books, 1984, p. 101). Destruction feeds on lust, lust on destruction—never a pure state, but at times chillingly close. This is veiled in much of life (thank God!), where there are openings for love, creative joy, and all the experiences that make living worthwhile. Still, there are many stories about the impossibility of keeping destruction hidden in a box outside of life. Psychoanalysis is one attempt, flawed but persistent, to search for ways to bring destruction out of boxes in ways that don't destroy.

p. 97: I. B. Singer (1992), *The Collected Stories*, New York: Noonday Press. For expressions of labyrinthine links between lust and delusion one can pull writers out of a hat: Philip Roth or Garbriel García-Marquez, for example. An overwhelming array of voices across the ages document intimacies between pleasure, joy, stupidity, fulfillment, disaster, and those omnipresent intertwining strands of the life pulse, hope and despair.

p. 97: clutching agony: see *Ecstasy*, pp. 64–66; *The Sensitive Self*, pp. 44–50.

p. 98: For the face as horizon or frame of reference or psychic organizer for body parts and functions, sentience, affect, aggressive and erotic surges, concupiscence, see my "face" papers in *The Electrified Tightrope*, chaps. 6–9; *The Sensitive Self*, chap. 11; *The Psychotic Core*, chaps. 4, 5, 7, and 8.

p. 99: "basic fault": M. Balint (1968), *The Basic Fault*, London: Routledge, 1979. Balint writes of a mar, a flaw or "fault"—something wrong with personality or the sense of self, like a fault line beneath the surface.

p. 99: where does the face go?: See note for p. 98.

p. 102: passionate dispassion: Meister Eckhart is one of the great examples; *Meister Eckhart* (1941), trans. R. B. Blakney, New York: Harper and Row.

p. 104: Socrates and Diotima: Plato's *Symposium*.

pp. 104–06: I. Kant (1983), *Perpetual Peace and Other Essays*, trans. T. Humphrey, Indianapolis: Hackett Publishing Company. Emmanuel Levinas, I believe, tells us something about the origin of the good *ought*, its embodiment or incarnation. He finds it in our response to the human face, an ethics of the face. The appeal, the vulnerability of the expressive face evokes in us a sense of justice, a wish, a drive, a need to do right by the other, a drive toward care and respect, an emotional field that bears goodness. Levinas describes an infinite appeal of the other, an appeal and response always beginning. E. Levinas (1969), *Totality and Infinity*, trans. A. Lingis, Pittsburgh: Duquesne University Press. A thread of developmental research, largely psychoanalytic, places a lot on the infant's (and mother's) sensitivity to facial expressiveness (e.g., Eigen, *The Electrified Tightrope*, chap. 6; H. Elkin [1972], "On Selfhood and the Development of Ego Structures in Infancy," *Psychoanalytic Review* 59:389–416; B. Beebe [2004], "Faces in Relation: A Case Study, *Psychoanalytic Dialogues* 14).

p. 105: *Equus* is a play by Peter Shaffer, popular in the early 1970s, in which a man struggles with his obsession with horses. The horse, incidentally, was a symbol of reason for Jonathan Swift, and is a body ego symbol in psychoanalysis, demonstrating cross-meanings of symbolic expressions, which often compress an intimacy of opposites.

About the author

MICHAEL EIGEN is in private practice in New York City. Author of numerous books, he is also Associate Clinical Professor of Psychology at New York University and a Senior Member at the National Psychological Association for Psychoanalysis. He has given a private weekly seminar on Wilfred Bion, Jacques Lacan, and D. W. Winnicott for more than thirty years and gives an online seminar on his own work. He is currently the editor of *The Psychoanalytic Review*.

Library of Congress
Cataloging-in-Publication Data
Eigen, Michael.
Lust / Michael Eigen.
p. cm.
Includes bibliographical references.
ISBN 0-8195-6808-2 (cloth : alk. paper)
—ISBN 0-8195-6809-0 (pbk. : alk. paper)
1. Sex. 2. Lust. I. Title.
HQ21.E325 2006
306.701—dc22
2005043469